*Leaving You*

# Leaving You

*The Cultural Meaning of Suicide*

## Lisa Lieberman

Ivan R. Dee

*Chicago*

2003

Library of Congress Cataloging-in-Publication Data:
Lieberman, Lisa J., 1956–
    Leaving you : the cultural meaning of suicide / Lisa Lieberman.
      p.   cm.
    Includes bibliographical references and index.
    ISBN 1-56663-496-2 (alk. paper)
     1. Suicide.   2. Self-destructive behavior.   I. Title.

HV6545 .L534 2003
362.28—dc21

2002041140

*To my father*

# Contents

|  | Preface | ix |
|---|---|---|
| 1 | Defiant Death | 3 |
| 2 | Death and Democracy | 38 |
| 3 | Sex and Suicide | 67 |
| 4 | Leaving You | 95 |
| 5 | Tragic Artists | 130 |
|  | Notes | 155 |
|  | Index | 167 |

# Preface

I CANNOT WRITE about suicide with perfect objectivity. At one time I would have considered this a weakness, my inability to approach the subject dispassionately, as if I had no stake in understanding what it meant. Trained as a European cultural historian, I cultivated a scientific detachment toward the past. Personal interest was suspect. The truths embedded within the documents pinned together in those dusty folders, the thick books, some with pages still uncut, that I read in the British Library and the French Bibliothèque Nationale, could not be extracted by a researcher encumbered with her own notions about self-destruction. Responsible historians checked their preconceptions, along with the rest of their personal baggage, at the door of the archives. The point was to rid yourself of bias— the beliefs, judgments, anxieties, hopes, and defenses that clouded your vision and rendered your findings invalid.

I found it safer to hold suicide at arm's length. And I was in good company. The nineteenth-century physicians, statisticians, moral reformers, and social critics whose works I studied were falling all over one another in their eagerness to come up with ways of explaining self-destruction that would remove its sting. They were quite open about what they feared. Suicide was an act of rebellion, in their eyes, a protest at once personal and political. In choosing to die, an individual severs the ties that bind him to others—to family, friends, and community. How could he leave us? survivors ask. If only we'd known, we could have helped. They feel betrayed and abandoned. Abandoned, but also accused. They did not know. They did not help. Now it is too late. What does it say about a society when its members choose, in ever-increasing numbers, to die? Is it not an indictment of the existing order and, if so, don't those who benefit from the status quo deserve a share of the blame?

Nineteenth-century observers did not so much explain as endeavor to explain away these disquieting considerations. But there were other questions they did not touch, questions posed most starkly in our own day by the suicides of Holocaust survivors. These deaths force us to examine our most comforting assumption about self-destruction: that individuals who kill themselves are entirely passive, that they do not seriously intend to die. My decision to frame this book with the suicides of three Holocaust survivors—Jean Améry in the beginning, Bruno Bettelheim and Primo Levi at the end—points up the error in this way of thinking. In public careers spanning thirty or forty years following their liberation from the camps, each struggled to regain the dignity he had lost at the hands of the Nazis. Our inclination to think of them still as Holocaust victims, our refusal to acknowledge that while they may have grown tired at the end, they nevertheless chose to leave the world, belittles all they managed to achieve in that time. Worse still, we risk turning them back into what the Nazis made them: victims with no control over their own destiny.

I came to appreciate the willfulness that self-destruction entails while volunteering some years ago as a counselor on a suicide hotline, listening to callers describe their reasons for wanting to die. But in a way I have always known it. Growing up with a mother who is a manic-depressive, aware that my grandfather, my father's father, had killed himself during the Great Depression, I was confronted by suicide from an early age. I never saw it as a helpless slide into oblivion; it was not that simple. Despair and anger, regrets and resentment were closely intertwined in my family history. My mother's threats were real, and yet, they were also a performance, her way (not a healthy way) of establishing her independence in the face of her illness and within a culture that did not offer enough to an intelligent woman of her generation.

Suicide is a painful topic, and I realize that my argument will make some readers uncomfortable. As a teacher I am committed to the give and take of discussion. My classrooms ring with debate. Here too I have chosen to present my views non-dogmatically, through a series of interwoven essays, each exploring a different dimension of self-destruction—a format that allows readers room for their own thoughts.

The thread that runs through all of them is my appreciation of self-destruction as a meaningful gesture, a statement that holds more than private significance. A statement, moreover, that is essentially subversive. At the very least, suicide is an expression of such profound isolation that our confidence in human relationships is shaken. But it is also an expression of autonomy: a flaunting of individualism that undermines social cohesion and threatens the foundation of public authority. This book charts the tension between society's interest in restraining suicide's disruptive power and the individual's freedom to determine the meaning of his own death.

The first three essays survey cultural attitudes toward self-destruction. In "Defiant Death" I trace the intellectual and historical currents that have served to deprive the act of significance, resulting in our modern-day tendency to view suicides as mere victims rather than acknowledging the authenticity of their intentions. "Death and Democracy" explores the political justification for patronizing, for treating as children, individuals who wish to die. To opt out of a system is effectively to condemn it; even the most oppressed members of society have the power to challenge its assumptions by voluntarily removing themselves from the community. The challenge posed by the suicide of the disfranchised is appraised more fully in "Sex and Suicide," an examination of the anxieties aroused by women's suicides in nineteenth-century Europe. In the final two essays I turn from an analysis of the discourse surrounding self-destruction to an investigation into the mentality of the so-called victims. "Leaving You" offers a critique of nineteenth-century narratives of suicidal despair and suggests how our own understanding of depression remains deeply imbued with the Romantic sensibility. The difficulties artists face in living up to our culture's expectations of the suffering artist and the salvation they hope to find in suicide is the subject of the last essay.

Portions of this book have appeared in different form in the

---

*Journal of Family History*, the *Gettysburg Review, Comparative Studies in Society and History*, and the *Oxford Companion to the Body*.

Many years of work and a lifetime of experiences, some very sad, have gone into this book. I could not have stayed the course without the unfailing love of my husband, Tim Lang. Peter Stitt gave me the confidence to venture beyond the realm of academic writing. I am also grateful to Jenene Allison, Victor Levine, Jo Margolis, Pernilla Neal, and Kim Rogers for their affectionate and stubborn support and to Angela Sellens Drake for keeping me whole in spirit. My father, Fred Lieberman, has been my best teacher. His belief in me has always been the source of my strength, but it is his sense of justice that has made me the person I am. I dedicate this book to him.

L. L.

*Norwich, England*
*February 2003*

To be solely a victim is not an honor.

Jean Améry

*Leaving You*

# ONE

# Defiant Death

Two years before he killed himself, the Austrian writer and Holocaust survivor Jean Améry described the aftermath of his first suicide attempt. "I still know very well how it was when I awoke after what was later reported to me as a thirty-hour coma," he told a German radio audience in 1976. "Fettered, drilled through with tubes, fitted on both wrists with painful devices for my artificial nourishment. Delivered and surrendered to a couple of nurses who came and went, washed me, cleaned my bed, put thermometers in my mouth, and did everything quite matter-of-factly, as if I were already a thing, *une chose*. . . . I was full of a deep bitterness against all those who meant well and had done this disgrace to me," Améry informed his listeners. "And I knew," he said, "better than ever before that I was inclined to die, and that the rescue, about which the physician boasted, belonged to the worst that had ever been done to me—and that was not a little."[1]

I have difficulty accepting Améry's resentment. Was his rescue really worse than being tortured by the Gestapo? Worse than two years in the death camps? Surely he did not mean to equate the minor indignities of the hospital routine with the calculated inhumanity of the Final Solution. Améry was neither terminally ill nor clinically depressed. He does not sound the way I would expect a person considering suicide to sound. His tone is reasonable, balanced, but unmovable, the anger fueled by a cold intelligence. "I bear my grudge for my personal salvation," he said.[2] The coldness is more unsettling than an emotional outburst, I think, because it repels any attempt at consolation. Améry is alone—dreadfully alone—but rather than trying to salve the wound of his isolation, he chooses to make the separation permanent. He is intent on leaving us, his audience, and I cannot help but feel implicated in his decision.

Améry's suicide was meant as a statement, a personal declaration of independence couched in the language of postwar French philosophy. His final radio address, "The Road to the Open," begins with the story of a prisoner confined to a cell so small that he cannot even pace it. From his barred window he watches the other prisoners taking their exercise in the fenced-in yard. The prisoner longs for the comparative freedom of the fenced-in yard. This is all he expects from life: the ability to walk for an hour or two within the barbed wire-enclosed space between the barracks. True liberation—life outside the prison walls—is inconceivable; he knows he will never see the outside world again. He has no hope of escaping his confinement except through death, but he is not ready to die. "[He] would still like to gulp down his evening soup and then the hot acorn soup in the morning and again a turnip soup at noon, and on and on."[3] He will settle for the "freedom" of the fenced-in yard.

Améry appreciated the prisoner's dilemma. He knew there was no such thing as absolute freedom. We are all constrained by birth and upbringing, customs, laws, and the day-to-day compromises we make in the course of a lifetime. Liberty, dignity, integrity: against these lovely abstractions are counterpoised the real activities of smiling, breathing, eating, the simple pleasure of taking a walk outdoors. Who are we to judge the prisoner? And yet Améry could not accept the prisoner's solution. He refused to live within the constraints imposed by society, refused to compromise his integrity for the sake of others or to give up on his struggle to reclaim the dignity he had lost at the hands of the Nazis. Only by voluntarily choosing to die could he resolve the impossible contradictions of his life. Suicide was not an act of self-annihilation, in his view, a passive succumbing to grief or despair; it was an active assertion of identity. "I die, therefore I am," he announced without a trace of irony.[4]

The philosophical tenor of Améry's radio addresses, his talk of freedom, choice, and authenticity—the favorite vocabulary of his mentor, Jean-Paul Sartre—might suggest that he too defined self-destruction purely in existentialist terms. But Améry regarded suicide as a political act: a protest whereby the victim ceases at last to be a victim by taking control of his own fate. In his introduction to a collection of photographs of the Warsaw ghetto published in 1969, he praised the resistance fighters "who took death into their own hands and, though powerless and unarmed, became avengers." Their heroism lay in their willingness to turn death into a form of revolt. The lesson of the Warsaw ghetto was revenge. "Here the redemptory application of violence had been found in its purest form," he wrote. "Here revenge was cleansed of a Christian moralism that was never able to prevent it, that always merely denied it. Here and here alone, as far as we can survey history, the dreadful and, in all its dreadfulness, empty phrase about 'cleansing the ignominy through blood' made good sense."[5]

Again I am uncomfortable with the harshness of Améry's position. His wholehearted endorsement of retributive justice scares me, and there is evidence that Améry himself came to regret his words in later years, when terrorist groups in Europe and the Middle East justified their activities in similar terms. The tone of his radio addresses became less provocative, less extreme, as if he were making a deliberate effort to be sensible and fair-minded, wanting to ensure that the meaning he placed on his own death would not be misconstrued. But the retaliatory nature of his suicide is unmistakable. "So farewell. I belong finally to myself," he declared.[6] On the night of October 17, 1978, Jean Améry shut himself in a Salzburg hotel room and took an overdose of prescription drugs. This time there were no rescuers.

I would prefer to bracket Améry's case, to dismiss his argument as irrelevant to my experience. His story was unique, after all, and thankfully so; few of us have suffered as he did. Still, a persistent voice in the back of my mind tells me that Améry was right about suicide. In a world indelibly altered by the rage of suicide bombers, who would deny that self-destruction can be both an act of aggression and a powerful public statement? The death desired, the ending sought, the final scene staged in the mind before it is performed, holds too much meaning to remain private. "Every suicide is a poem sublime in its melancholy," Balzac remarked in *La Peau de chagrin*.[7] Melancholic or angry, cowardly or heroic: suicide is a statement that cries out to be deciphered, yet the cultural history of self-destruction consists of a series of attempts to evade this truth by depriving suicide of its broader implications.

Efforts to read meaning out of suicide are not hard to find today. Therapeutic strategies that treat suicide as an illness, medicating the depression while ignoring the underlying motivations that drive people to end their lives, effectively diminish individual responsibility for the decision to die. In a similar way, sociological explanations that emphasize social causes over personal intentions serve to make suicides passive: victims of forces beyond their control—forces that can, reassuringly, be isolated and manipulated by the sociologist. But an appreciation of the disruptive potential of self-destruction, the power of individuals to use death as a weapon in order to undermine the authority of states or to bring into question the cherished values of societies and institutions, pervades the Western tradition.

Witness the death of Socrates, at one and the same time the ultimate symbol of obedience to state authority and a powerful challenge to the legitimacy of that authority. Socrates was arrested and brought to trial on the charge of corrupting the minds of Athenian youth in 399 B.C. Plato's dramatization of the trial, the *Apology*, portrays Socrates in a noble light; his stubborn restatement of his position in the face of the prosecution's case against him, his unwillingness to surrender his self-appointed role as gadfly in Athenian society, challenging all he meets to examine their consciences, even when it is made clear to him that the penalty for continuing in this behavior is death: all are evidence of high moral seriousness.

But Plato also provides evidence that Socrates wanted to die. In the *Crito*, Socrates turns down his friends' offer to help him escape from prison, claiming that he would no longer merit their respect were he so blatantly to disobey the laws of his society, however unfair they may appear—and he never denies that he has been unjustly condemned to death. But having chosen to live in Athens for his entire life and benefited from its civic institutions, he feels he must abide by its codes. A religious motivation is introduced with the *Phaedo*, where Socrates justifies his willingness to let the state put him to death by insisting it is the gods' decision that he do so. Here he also manages to represent voluntary death as a means of preserving his self-respect. "I should only make myself ridiculous in my own eyes if I clung to life and hugged it when it has no more to offer," he consoles his followers as he prepares to drink the hemlock.[8]

The ambiguities inherent in Socrates' death are as striking today as they must have been to Plato's audience in the fourth century B.C. Commentators on the *Apology* are divided over whether Socrates deserved to die for corrupting the minds of Athenian youth. Some find him arrogant and consider the Socratic method a real danger to public authority. Others admire Socrates for his refusal to give in, regarding him as the victim of a corrupt system of justice. But all agree that Plato's rendering of the event transformed Socrates into a hero. Like Samson, who pulled the temple of the Philistines down upon his enemies and himself—so the dead whom he slew at his death were more than those whom he had slain during his life—Socrates' suicide was a triumph. As a statement, it spoke more eloquently than any of the words he uttered in his trial, a lesson that was not lost on Jean Améry.

Dignity and integrity; a heroic sacrifice apparently undertaken with divine sanction; a protest at once personal and political, carrying a hint of posthumous revenge: all are discernable in Socrates' suicide, and these themes would resonate over the centuries. The death of Socrates seemed to embody both reason and self-control, qualities prized by the early Stoics, and euthanasia was practiced among elderly members of the school. In theory, suicide was an option available to the Stoic at any time. In practice, however, only the first-century statesman and philosopher Seneca glorified death to the point of advocating self-destruction as an end in itself. His own suicide at the command of the emperor Nero was supposedly consistent with the principles he espoused. The story goes that he managed to stretch the event over the course of an entire day, drinking wine and conversing with his friends while periodically opening his veins until he eventually bled to death.

Seneca's willingness to "end his career" in cold blood earned the admiration of his contemporaries. And his was but one of the many heroic suicides that have come down to us from Roman antiquity. Lucretia killed herself because she was raped by Sextus Tarquinius; Cato chose death over defeat in battle; Brutus took his life when the cause of the Republic was lost, and his wife, Portia, swallowed hot coals upon hearing a rumor of his death; Mark Antony, believing Cleopatra was dead, stabbed himself after being beaten by Caesar's forces; unwilling to survive her lover or to be taken prisoner, Cleopatra cut short her existence by applying an asp to her breast.

The legends of Lucretia, Seneca, Cato, Brutus, Portia, Antony, and Cleopatra inspired elegies, plays, and works of art throughout the centuries. Their deaths became models for a distinctive subgenre within the annals of self-destruction: the suicide of honor. To die for some higher ideal, for the sake of virtue, patriotism, or faith, was to turn death into an occasion for homage. Suicide purified the defiled and ennobled the enemy of the state, made a martyr of the heretic and a victor of the vanquished. The early Christians who chose death over lives of pagan dishonor clearly appreciated the symbolic value of the public execution. While the church fathers publicly maintained that fleeing persecution instead of martyring oneself might have been the better course, few of them saw these deaths as anything other than noble sacrifices. Indeed, the early church made a virtue of such manifestations of worldly detachment and stubborn faith. So great was the appeal of the heroic mode of self-destruction that the church was eventually forced to formulate a policy against it. Beginning with the fourth-century Donatists, Christians who actively sought death for any reason were denied burial in sacred ground.

The Christian case against suicide was formally stated by Saint Augustine, who prohibited the act on the grounds that it violated the sixth commandment: Thou shalt not murder. But Augustine was in fact ambivalent on the question of suicide. Vestiges of his youthful love of Plato, which he never wholly renounced, led him, like Socrates, to permit it in those instances where individuals behaved with divine sanction in putting an end to their lives. "To kill oneself at God's command is not suicide," he asserted.[9] This refinement was necessary in order to allow for the voluntary sacrifice of Jesus, who freely chose to die on the cross for the sins of humanity, while at the same time excluding Judas, who hanged himself in despair, violating the divine will.

What I find most significant about Augustine's attempt to recast suicide as an act of murder is that it effectively altered the terms by which self-destruction was judged, supplanting the Roman ideal of heroic individualism with a Platonic concept of submission to divine authority, with all the ambiguities this concept implied. That such an alteration was desired in the fifth century reveals a great deal about the changed status of Christianity at this time. Augustine was born forty years after the Emperor Constantine's conversion and lived to see his faith adopted as the official religion of the Roman Empire. No longer a besieged institution struggling to maintain its existence in a hostile world, the church was then engaged in the task of consolidating its hold over its own adherents. The future of Christianity depended on its ability to overcome the dissension within its own ranks. Against this background, the meaning of suicide was transformed. Where martyrdom once served as a symbol of personal integrity, it was now seen as an act of rebellion against legitimate authority.

The church policy regarding suicide that emerged during the Middle Ages was loosely based on Roman law. Following ancient Greek traditions, the Romans had punished self-destruction, but only under certain conditions: when an individual killed himself to escape legal prosecution or in the case of a soldier or a slave. The act of suicide was not itself considered blameworthy. Rather, the suicide's civil status combined with his presumed motivations—the cowardliness of the accused man who sought to preempt the law, the disobedience of the soldier, or the audacity of the slave who disposed of a life that was not truly his—determined whether the act should be punished.

The Christian position was different. What made suicide a sin was its voluntary nature. Self-destruction was prohibited because it represented an individual's choice to do wrong, a deliberate challenge to divine authority. Following the publication of the *Summa Theologiae* of Thomas Aquinas, suicide came to be seen as a crime against society as well. Aristotle had condemned suicide on political grounds, arguing that the allegiance individuals owed to the state precluded them from taking their lives. Aquinas revived Aristotle's view of suicide as an act of political insubordination and also criticized self-destruction on the grounds that it went against the natural instinct for self-preservation. To the traditional religious objection, which served to deny the sinner a Christian burial, Aquinas thus added a provision that could be used to support the implementation of civil penalties against people who killed themselves. During the High Middle Ages, civil legislation against self-murder was enacted in the majority of Western European states. Not only was it forbidden to kill yourself but also to put yourself in a position where the likelihood of death at the hands of another was high, such as engaging in a tournament or a duel. This was considered indirect suicide and punished by depriving the suicide of the right to burial in sanctified ground. Under no circumstances were men or women permitted to sacrifice themselves without divine sanction or to place their own needs above the needs of the community to which they belonged.

This prohibition was not actually as harsh as it might seem, for there were always ways of evading the penalties against suicide. For example, when it was unclear whether a given death was intentional or accidental, the usual presumption was that an accident had occurred. Sympathy for the surviving family or outright bribery also seems to have influenced church officials in many instances to declare that an individual had been of unsound mind at the time he or she attempted to die. But political events that forced individuals to redefine their relationship to political and religious authority had the effect of contravening this tolerant practice because of the defiant implications of removing oneself from the community. Augustine's attempt to redefine suicide during a time of social upheaval, when barbarian invasions and internal disorder threatened to destroy the Roman Empire, was therefore not unique. The English Reformation, a period of religious change and political instability, also sparked a transformation in the official policy toward self-destruction, but the change in this instance proved to be temporary.

By the end of the Middle Ages, instances of profane burial and posthumous legal prosecution had become rare in England, though the crime of self-murder would remain a punishable offense until 1823. Beginning in the mid-1500s, however, suicide was interpreted as a sign of diabolic possession in the British Isles, heightening fears and strengthening the grounds for repressing the act. For a period of about a century, popular superstitions, Christian doctrine, and civil legislation were united as church and state worked together to extend their influence over the people. The laws against self-murder were rigorously applied, bodies were desecrated, and it became common practice for the suicide's goods to be confiscated by the crown. Even the number of suicides being reported increased significantly as magistrates sought to make an example of those individuals who defied the state's power. Verdicts of unsound mind became the exception. Only with the resolution of the religious crisis after the English Civil War did the harsh policy toward the crime of self-destruction again soften. By the end of the seventeenth century, England had become an increasingly secular, politically stable society, and with these developments came a renewed willingness to attribute suicide to mental impairment.[10]

Suicide's prominence as a religious and judicial issue sparked interest in the moral implications of self-destruction. *Biathanatos*, the treatise written in 1602 by John Donne, the English poet and dean of St. Paul's, was the most famous contribution to this literature. "Whensoever any affliction assails me, methinks I have the keys of my prison in mine own hand," he wrote, "and no remedy presents itself so soon to my heart as mine own sword."[11] Few English thinkers went so far as Donne in defending suicide. Donne himself seems to have had second thoughts about the enterprise; *Biathanatos* was not published until after his death. But the seventeenth century did evince a willingness to debate the issue and to subject the certainties of the theologians to rational scrutiny. At the same time, the revival of classical antiquity initiated during the Renaissance and continuing into this period brought a new appreciation for the arguments of the Stoics and for the heroic Roman tradition. Shakespeare's tragedies presented suicide in sympathetic terms: Hamlet's soliloquy, Othello's remorse, the madness of Lear and Ophelia, the poignant deaths of the lovers Romeo and Juliet, the noble endings of Brutus, Antony, and Cleopatra still have the power to move us.

A more lasting redefinition of the meaning of suicide occurred in France during the late eighteenth century, becoming

a battle that raged until the eve of World War I. It was here
that our own understanding of voluntary death was forged. Literary models and statistical studies, sociological theories and
psychiatric assumptions, including the popular notion that people "succumb" to their self-destructive urges—the victim-
oriented approach to suicide that Jean Améry so vehemently
opposed—all developed in response to the fear engendered by
the French Revolution. Viewed symbolically, suicide was an
abuse of liberty, an act of revolt; as such, it posed a threat to
public order. At a time when liberty was seen as problematic,
efforts to play down the defiance implied in the act of self-
destruction took on new urgency. In fact, the origins of this
particular contest over suicide's significance must be sought in
the *ancien régime* debates over individual rights versus monar-
chical authority and in the struggle of radical philosophers to
create a secular state.

The Ordinance of 1670 codified the religious prohibitions
against suicide into French law. By its terms, criminal proceed-
ings were instituted against the cadaver or against the memory
of individuals who killed themselves. The stated penalty was
confiscation of the suicide's property. Additionally, the body was
to be dragged, face down, through the streets on a hurdle and
hanged by the feet as a public example. In 1712 and again in
1736, the terms of the ordinance were reiterated and strengthened in royal declarations calling for surgical autopsies, the ques-
tioning of witnesses in cases where suicide was suspected, and
the forbidding of burial until the question had been resolved.

Over the course of the eighteenth century, suicide became
a matter of public dispute, largely owing to the polemical writings of the *philosophes* and to the publicity surrounding such

*causes célèbres* as the Calas affair. In 1762 a Protestant merchant, Jean Calas, was convicted by the *parlement* of Toulouse for murdering his son, who had supposedly wished to convert to Catholicism. Calas was tortured to death on the wheel, his broken body was burned to ashes, and his remaining son was banished from the country. Voltaire's well-publicized investigation into the case revealed that Calas had been wrongly accused. The grieving father's only crime had been to attempt to hide the evidence of his son's suicide in order to spare his family from the humiliation of the reigning penal procedures.

By the time Calas was formally exonerated in 1765, the issue had assumed major proportions in France. Critics of the *ancien régime* found in the harsh legislation against self-destruction an effective means of undermining the divine source of the king's authority. Recalling the arguments of the sixteenth-century essayist Michel de Montaigne, which represented the decision to die as a personal choice, Enlightenment thinkers questioned the legitimacy of extending civic legislation into the realm of religious beliefs. Was it appropriate for the law to be used in enforcing Christian virtue, they asked, or were these matters not better left to God? In terms of strategy, the *philosophes'* question was a brilliant maneuver. Although seeming to give ground to the traditional religious interpretation of suicide, it actually succeeded in shifting the debate onto a different plane. The moral implications of self-destruction were now set aside; whether or not suicide was a sin did not interest the *philosophes*, whose concerns were wholly secular. Instead they reaffirmed suicide's significance as a political act: a proud affirmation of personal freedom.[12]

This appeal to the Stoic image of self-destruction was quite

deliberate. The *philosophes* set out to revitalize the pagan tradition, embracing the materialist doctrines of antiquity in their
crusade against Christianity and contrasting the glorious Roman
republic with the bankruptcy of Bourbon absolutism. Voltaire
and others immortalized the great Roman poets in the name of
rationalism and freedom, portraying Lucretius, Cicero, and Seneca—all apologists of the right to die—as early upholders of
their cause. In his famous history, Montesquieu suggested that
the willingness of Roman heroes to die for the sake of liberty
accounted, at least in part, for their greatness. The example of
Cato, who watched his followers sail off to safety and then
calmly stabbed himself in lieu of surrendering to Caesar's forces,
was frequently invoked by advocates of a republican form of
government in France.[13] And in the *Persian Letters*, Montesquieu
explicitly portrayed suicide as an act of rebellion against unrea-
sonable authority. "I may have lived in servitude, but I have
always been free," the odalisque Roxana writes to Usbek from
the seraglio. "I have amended your laws according to the laws
of nature, and my mind has always remained independent." As
the poison she swallowed begins to take effect, she dares to
address her master as an equal: "Such language is new to you,
no doubt. Is it possible that after having overwhelmed you with
grief, I could force you to admire my courage?"[14]

More sensationally, during the darkest days of the French
Revolution numerous revolutionaries took their lives in self-
conscious imitation of Cato. The Ordinance of 1670 was over-
turned by the Constitutional Assembly in 1790, and the Penal
Code of 1791 did not include suicide among its enumerations
of crimes. But beginning under the Terror in 1793, the heroic
Roman mode of death grew so popular among jailed opponents

of Robespierre's regime that the penalties against self-destruction were reinstated.[15] Naturally, the significance of this correlation—that the revolutionaries should have resorted to suicide when overwhelmed by events they themselves had unleashed—did not go unnoticed by the right. To all who longed for a return to the *ancien régime*, the cult of antiquity initiated by the *philosophes* and carried to an extreme by the men of 1793 represented a dire foreshadowing of the nation's fate. Like Rome, France appeared to be crumbling from within, adrift intellectually, ridden with vice, and plagued with political instability. In this setting, self-destruction seemed less an affirmation of personal freedom than a manifestation of national despair.

Throughout the nineteenth century, conservatives invoked the fall of Rome as a metaphor for the postrevolutionary age. Suicide was portrayed as the inevitable consequence of the immoral extravagance that had characterized Imperial Rome. Death lurked behind the opulent façades of marble and gold and was never far from the scene of that most Roman of entertainments, the orgy. For in time even the greatest hedonist tired of overindulging in physical pleasures. Sensuality, gluttony, and limitless wealth eventually lost their charms, and the dissipated Roman was left to brood upon the emptiness of the remaining days of his life. "According to the pace by which the times advance toward decline, the number of suicides multiplies without measure," noted a professor of literature in 1869. "Strange contrast to which the history of all civilizations, worn out by their own excesses, has accustomed us!"[16]

Support for the right-wing case was derived from the official statistics, which showed that the annual rate of suicides was rising more steeply than the growth of the French population. There are good grounds to question the reliability of these statistics, particularly since they had only begun to be compiled systematically in 1827, and indeed, there were writers who warned that the figures should be approached with caution. But even taking the available statistical information with a degree of skepticism, the fact remains that at no time during the nineteenth century did France have the highest per capita rate of voluntary deaths. That distinction was held by Denmark until the mid-1860s and by Saxony thereafter. If France's suicide rate was increasing, so were those of other industrializing nations, as anyone who cared to consult the comparative findings of the Belgian statistician Adolphe Quetelet could have discovered.

Yet the nineteenth-century French were convinced they were living in the midst of an epidemic of self-inflicted death, which they traced directly to the Revolution and to the dangerous hopes it inspired. Already in 1820 the physician Pierre Reydellet had written, "I would not hesitate to attribute the multitude of suicides now taking place in France to the birth of liberty in this country." In his 1827 study of French morality from the reign of Louis XVI through the accession of Charles X, Antoine Caillot blamed the revolutionaries for instilling "a ferocious passion for liberty and equality" among the lower classes. A literary critic echoed Caillot's concern in 1845. A veritable *manie du suicide* was cultivated among the Stoic and Epicurean sects, claimed Saint-Marc Girardin. "And if, in our day, artisans are, alas, themselves afflicted with the suicide malady," he lamented, "that only goes to show that their spirits are being ceaselessly vexed and embittered by the teachings of our modern civilization." It was the *philosophes'* substitution of materialist philosophy for Christian ethics, according to Girardin, to which the majority of suicides could be attributed.[17]

Conservatives did not hold exclusive rights to the Rome analogy in nineteenth-century France. Liberals and socialists were just as likely to invoke the declining empire in the course of their own social critiques. No less prominent figures than the Orleanist politician François Guizot and the great liberal historian Jules Michelet published works in the 1830s and '40s comparing their nation to Rome. Socialists such as Constantin Pecqueur and Charles Fourier also stressed the similarities between their own society's degeneration and Rome's fall. Among liberal and left-wing writers, however, self-destruction sustained its heroic connotations. "In times of decadence, when the fire of patriotism and of liberty is extinguished and tyrants reign," a pseudonymous writer of republican proclivities remarked in 1842,

> public spirit flickers like a dying person who revives a few times before taking his last breath. Those in whom the sacred fire survives, when finding themselves in the midst of such corruption, cowardice, infamy, fall into despair. In such a state they often have no other desire than to follow the decline of their age. This accounts for the suicides of many ancient and modern heroes.[18]

The nineteenth-century controversy over the meaning of suicide was really about France's political future. As a result of the *philosophes'* arguments and the popularity of the classical mode of self-destruction during the Terror, suicide had regained its symbolic status as an act of protest, but the legitimacy of this protest depended on where the writer stood on the political spectrum. Spiritual descendants of the *philosophes* and others who upheld the legacy of the Revolution saw suicide as an act of dignity, an affirmation of personal freedom. Those who sought to return France to her religious and political traditions continued to view self-destruction as an abuse of liberty, the assertion of individual will against public authority.

In either case, the troubling increase in the suicide rate suggested that the grounds for the protest were not adequately being addressed. Suicide was now seen as a problem existing somewhere along a continuum of subversive gestures that ran from individual challenges to public order such as crime to collective manifestations of unrest such as revolutionary violence, a dilemma neatly conceptualized in 1840 by a Dijon philosophy professor. "After having broken so violently with the past, knowing neither what to love nor what to believe, lost in the present and frightened of a future that already seems dark," wrote Joseph Tissot, "the weak man kills himself." Under similar circumstances, another individual might turn to violence instead of succumbing to his despair, directing his anger outward against the government or the society he held responsible for his unhappiness.[19] Finding a resolution to this problem—a means of combating the despair and anger that threatened the stability of the nation—became the mission of French alienists and moral statisticians, crusaders in the professions today known as psychiatry and sociology. While they pursued different strategies, reformers in both fields achieved the same results. Their theories had the effect of divesting individuals of responsibility for antisocial behavior, placing power in the hands of specialists at the expense of personal autonomy.

The conservative agenda that underlay the development of

the mental health profession in France has been the subject of both scholarly interest and popular debate over the past forty years.[20] Owing to the Revolution, to the complete overhaul of the bureaucracy begun in 1789 and consolidated under Napoleon, everything from the training and licensing of physicians to the supervision of hospitals and asylums was placed under government control. The revolutionaries assumed responsibility for the nation's health: the physical, mental, and moral well-being of their fellow citizens. Sickness and insanity were combated not merely, as in the *ancien régime*, because they posed a threat to public order. Such afflictions undermined the very principles upon which the French Republic was founded. Democracy. Liberty. Each required the contribution of an enlightened populace, citizens capable of recognizing the responsibilities that freedom entailed. To create individuals sound of body and mind, individuals capable of exercising their rights and participating responsibly in political life, became the joint project of the medical community and the state.

Was it merely a coincidence that the interests of physicians and the state should have converged at the time of the Revolution, at just the moment in France's history when Marxists claim that the bourgeoisie—the social class to which the majority of physicians belonged—was assuming power in political affairs? This question is at the heart of the anti-psychiatry movement, an attack on the repressive function of the mental health system that came to prominence during the May 1968 demonstrations. Along with the students who built barricades in the Latin Quarter and occupied university buildings, and the two million French workers who went out on strike, radical physicians seized control of medical facilities in Paris and attempted to make the profession more liberal and democratic by dismantling its hierarchical structure. Not only did the demonstrators attack the practice of medicine, their aim was to bring down the entire white-collar establishment. "This civilization is the disguise that permanent repression assumes in order to conceal and perpetuate itself," the young doctors proclaimed in their manifesto. "Because as a rule this repression does not have the obvious shiny appearance of a helmeted gendarme, but that of less shocking, more acceptable uniforms, ones that are often even desired, such as a doctor's smock or a professor's cap and gown."

Of particular concern to the demonstrators were the abuses of psychiatric power within the asylum regime. These abuses had been chronicled by the unorthodox historian Michel Foucault in two works dating from the early 1960s, *Birth of the Clinic* and *Madness and Civilization*. Much like Thomas Szasz in the United States and R. D. Laing in Great Britain, Foucault examined the assumptions that justified the incarceration of certain individuals—the "mentally ill"—for the good of society. By analyzing the language the early psychiatrists employed, the metaphors that hardened into the diagnostic categories we employ today, he showed how the mental health profession acquired its authoritative position over the course of the late eighteenth and nineteenth centuries.

Psychiatry emerged very slowly as a distinct discipline within medicine. Psychiatric training for medical students in France did not entail a separate curriculum until well after 1850, which means that the majority of physicians who wrote on suicide during this period approached the subject from a physiological perspective, applying their understanding of bodily ailments to the uncharted domain of the mind. The apparent epidemic of self-destruction was ideally suited to their orienta-tion; indeed, many doctors seemed to regard suicide, literally, as a contagious disease. This inclination is hardly surprising in an age when the ravages of cholera, smallpox, typhoid, and typhus fever were still being felt, and when suicides often seemed to occur in clusters, like viral outbreaks. But the phy-sicians' strategy had a political dimension as well. Heirs to the anti-clerical *philosophes*, the early psychiatrists were struggling to wrest the care of the mentally ill from religious orders, pitting reason against faith, science against superstition. Evaluating su-icide not in terms of morality but as a product of mental illness provided them with a means of undermining the cherished val-ues of Christianity. For if anyone who committed suicide was unhealthy, what was the status of the early Christian saints and martyrs, whose noble sacrifices had inspired countless acts of devotion?

In his two-volume work on insanity, the physician Louis Florentin Calmeil sketched the historical record of dementia, monomania, hallucinations, and other manifestations of madness from the fifteenth century through the present. Religious vision and frenzies seemed to interest him most, and, not surprisingly, much of what Calmeil wrote seems to have been intended for anti-clerical use. For example, after a paragraph mentioning bib-lical prophecies, saints' visions, and the mystical cults of the Middle Ages, he moved on to describe the delusions he had observed among the patients at the asylum of Charenton, bridg-ing the two discussions with the following comment: "One is tempted to take pity on the human species when one probes to the source, which is often puerile, of the very institutions, be-liefs and events which dominate, govern and inspire a society from its earliest beginnings." Obviously such a conclusion troubled his Catholic colleagues. "I cannot bring myself to believe," wrote the physician Gustave François Etoc-Demazy, "that [suicide] is always and necessarily an instance of mental alienation." As he went on to argue, "Surely God would not wish us to regard Saint Dominic and Saint Pelagius, who voluntarily took their own lives, as nothing more than monomaniacs."[21]

The problem for Christian apologists like Etoc-Demazy was how to distinguish the willful martyrdom of the saint from the cowardly exit of ordinary souls. By attributing self-destruction to some sort of mental imbalance, psychiatrists blurred the distinction between moral and immoral behavior. What was the virtue, after all, in succumbing to a mad impulse? One could hardly revere a lunatic. Nor could a person who was mentally ill be held accountable for his actions. But however troubling the psychiatric approach to the problem of self-destruction may have been on a spiritual level, its political use was invaluable. The diagnoses of the French alienists effectively neutralized the threat that suicide represented to social stability, discrediting the act by removing its heroic connotations. The test of their success would come at mid-century, when a maverick physician took on the greatest hero France had ever known: Emperor Napoleon Bonaparte.

While still a young lieutenant, Napoleon had been influenced by his reading of Romantic literature to compose some poignant pages of his own. In his essay on suicide, written in May 1786 when he was just seventeen, patriotic laments over the degradation of his native Corsica mingle with sentimental expressions of loneliness and self-pity, as in the following passage: "So, what fury leads me to desire my own destruction? It is the question, 'What is there for me to do in this world?' Since I have to die, I might as well kill myself." Before long, Napoleon would discover his vocation and achieve the domination of France over much of Europe, if not the liberation of Corsica from French rule. But suicide remained an option in times of despair. After the siege of Toulon in 1793, and again on the eve of his first abdication at Fontainebleau in 1814, following the surrender of Paris, he attempted to end his life.[22]

Interest in the emperor's suicide attempts was sparked by the publication in 1842 of excerpts from the young Napoleon's journal in the prominent literary magazine *Revue des deux mondes*. Evidence of the Toulon and Fontainebleau episodes had come to light a year earlier, when General Montholon's memoirs recounting the final years of the defeated hero appeared in print. In both cases care was taken to present the events in a flattering way. The portrait Montholon draws of his commander, discouraged in his hopes for a future but willing to sacrifice his dream of personal grandeur for the sake of his country, was meant to elicit sympathy and admiration. "Exhausted by this struggle of my mind, a mind French in every feeling, and faithful to my oath," Napoleon is supposed to have said, "I gave up that crown which I had only accepted for the glory and prosperity of France." In this frame of mind, he swallowed the poison he had carried in a pouch around his neck since the Russian campaign— but discovered that it had lost its strength in the intervening years. "It was not God's will that I should die so soon. . . . St. Helena was in my destiny."[23]

To Charles Bourdin, a physician writing near the end of the 1840s, Napoleon's suicide attempts constituted prima facie evidence that this man, considered for so many years to be a hero, was in fact insane. In Bourdin's opinion, someone who tried to kill himself, regardless of his motives or historical reputation, was not acting in full possession of his reason. Bourdin went on to assert that heroes, as a group, showed a higher statistical inclination toward insanity than the general population. "I state this without malicious intent," he wrote; "we are dealing with pure science, after all, and not with political satire."[24] Bourdin's scientific detachment was not appreciated by all his colleagues, but his conception of the relationship between suicide and insanity was hardly new. The famous pioneer in the field of mental alienation, J. E. D. Esquirol, in an article published in 1821 in a medical encyclopedia, had described suicide as a symptom of mental disorders.[25] Throughout the century, newspapers popularized medical theories, employing definitions drawn from the works of prominent physicians in their reports of sensational crimes and suicides. *La République*, a radical journal that appeared during France's short-lived attempt to establish a socialist republic, prefaced the tale of a young woman's suicide with the observation that she had shown signs of mental illness before the event. During the reign of Napoleon III a conservative newspaper printed stories of tragic accidents, immoral activities, and the "suicide monomania" alongside its religious and political commentary. By the end of the century, medical terminology had permeated the language that laymen used to discuss mental and social disorders. When *La Petite république*, a left-wing daily published at the turn of the century, attributed suicide in its columns to "mental alienation" or a "fatal hereditary disposition," it was simply following a well-established precedent.[26]

On the surface, the shift from the harsh *ancien régime* prohibitions against suicide to the therapeutic understanding of self-destruction that gained currency over the course of the nineteenth century was a sign of progress. No longer ostracized by the church and subject to legal punishment, individuals who attempted to end their own lives were not considered evil. They were simply sick. Sick people deserved compassion, not blame; with treatment, they could be cured. But the consequence of removing morality from the equation was that it also removed volition. Presuming that no one in his or her right mind wanted to die, psychiatrists felt no qualms about disregarding the stated motivations of potential suicides in order to rid them of their delusions. The case studies published by French alienists during this period are filled with tricks: manipulative strategies designed to bring crazy people back to their senses. From the patient's point of view, it is unclear whether the dispassionate psychiatric approach to self-destruction was an improvement over the value-laden perspective of earlier eras. What was healthy was surely good, after all, whereas to treat suicide as a sign of illness was still to stigmatize it as an evil.

Describing a patient whose state of mental deterioration had progressed from masturbation to delirium, culminating in an attempt to take his own life, a Dr. Biaute outlined the course of treatment he had employed to restore the man to health. At the time G. was placed under Biaute's care, he had already tried to kill himself but did not exhibit what Biaute considered to be the "normal" symptoms of mental illness, complaining only of physical ailments that appeared to be occasioned by the "sinister habit" in which he indulged. In order to impede him from masturbating and to prevent him from making another attempt at suicide, G. was forced to wear a linen belt attaching his wrists to either side of his body. As soon as this remedy was applied,

Biaute noted, G.'s condition began to improve. He complained less and showed fewer signs of delirium; on some visits, Biaute found him smiling, "appearing to be ashamed of his vice." Although G. asked repeatedly to have the belt removed, Biaute left it in place for two months, not wishing, he said, to compromise the success of his cure. The article in which he published his account concludes on a defensive note. "Finally, I would like to state that the method of restraint which I employed for a relatively long period of time was necessary; the results prove it," Biaute asserted, adding that no judge could possibly accuse him of surpassing the bounds of humane treatment.[27]

The measures Biaute employed in his treatment of G., though hardly unique for the period,[28] represent an extreme in the psychiatrists' efforts to impose their understanding of the relationship between suicide and insanity upon a captive population. What I find most striking about this case history is Biaute's attitude. In his arrogant disregard for his patient's wishes, his half-conscious admission that he had violated G's dignity, it is easy to see what infuriated Améry about his own rescue. Whether viewed as victims of diabolical possession or prey to the demons of mental illness, individuals at risk of destroying themselves were deprived of the right to determine their own behavior. "Delivered and surrendered to a couple of nurses who came and went, washed me, cleaned my bed, put thermometers in my mouth, and did everything quite matter-of-factly, as if I were already a thing, *une chose*. . . ." Jean Améry was treated like a thing because he was presumed to be mentally unstable. The evident seriousness of his intention to die became the justification for not taking him seriously.

Liberty, self-determination, free will—cherished values of Western society—all depend on a conception of personal autonomy that the psychiatric approach to suicide effectively denies, and this is true regardless of whether mental illness is treated as the product of psychological trauma or of some neurobiological imbalance. A similar restriction of individual freedom characterizes the sociological approach to self-destruction, and here too it was in nineteenth-century France that the foundation for our modern understanding was laid.

French sociology developed from three sources: philosophy, the physical sciences, and statistics. Because the classical orientation of the French university system distinguished sharply between science and the humanities, the social sciences emerged as subdisciplines within history, pedagogy, and philosophy. Education in the humanities was grounded in philosophical training until well after World War I, which accounts for the speculative flavor of French social scientific thought to this very day. But it had been the intention of the founder of sociology, Auguste Comte, to combine a philosophical understanding of behavior with a methodology drawn from the physical sciences. Comte proposed that observation take the place of abstract hypotheses in explaining social phenomena. Although he never succeeded in ridding his science of its unscientific elements, his philosophical lectures on "social physics," or "sociology," as he chose to rename it in 1839, set the tone for future investigations not only in his native country but in England, Germany, Belgium, and the United States.

Comte's empirical agenda coincided with the project of the Marquis de Laplace, the French astronomer and mathematician whose 1812 treatise on probability theory launched the new science of moral statistics. Probability theory would provide reasonable grounds for scientific investigations into the realm of human behavior, where subjective considerations must take the place of experimental verification. In the absence of hard data, Laplace believed that hypotheses based upon numerous observations of social phenomena could be generalized into laws, which might then be used to explain and predict events of moral and political significance. Statistics on mortality, population size, and income had been collected by the French government from the late sixteenth century for purposes of security and taxation. Following the popularization of Laplace's work, public statistics were standardized into a science, providing for the collection and analysis of data with mathematical precision. Beginning in 1827, national figures on social conditions such as poverty, crime, and suicide began to appear, published annually in the *Compte générale de la justice criminelle en France.*

The first moral statisticians to apply Laplace's theory, Adolphe Quetelet and A. M. Guerry, set themselves the task of defining the scope and limits of quantitative social analysis. Quetelet was introduced to the French work on probabilities in 1823, when he studied under Laplace and J. B. J. Fourier at the Ecole Polytechnique. Until this point he had been a mathematics professor in Brussels, though it was his interest in building a Belgian observatory that drew him to Paris. Statistics provided a means of applying his knowledge of mathematical principles and the abstract reasoning he had learned from astronomy toward a more practical end: the examination of social anatomy. The most significant aspect of his program was the emphasis he placed on external factors over internal motivations in determining human behavior. Free will was not excluded from his calculations but, like any variable, it could be corrected for, if not precisely measured, in the broader context of social laws. And suicide served as the perfect illustration of Quetelet's claims. This act "which appears so intimately connected with volition," manifested a striking regularity in its occurrence when examined collectively, he asserted. Without denying the particular circumstances that might lead an individual to take his own life, Quetelet managed to demonstrate, by means of statistical compilations, that the event was governed by the same general laws of recurrence as any material phenomenon.[29] Sixty years later, Emile Durkheim would make the identical point in his classic study of self-destruction, Le Suicide.

Durkheim also drew heavily on the findings of A. M. Guerry. A lawyer by profession, Guerry was primarily interested in discovering the correlation between education, religion, and crime. His 1833 Essai sur la statistique morale de la France began promisingly enough with the assertion that "the facts of the moral order must submit, like those of the physical order, to invariable laws," but soon turned into a critique of industrial development and city life. Guerry's argument drew its strength from the statistical correlation he claimed to have discovered between self-destruction and the corrupting influence of the urban milieu. "Among the influences [on suicide rates] that we have been considering," he wrote, "there is none more remarkable than that of the proximity to Paris." The conclusion he drew from this evidence—that improvements in education and industrial development must proceed hand in hand with religious instruction—seemed to be confirmed by the findings of subsequent researchers. In fact, scant data existed on suicide rates beyond the Paris region at the time the Essai appeared; it was largely on the basis of Guerry's recommendations that the Ministry of Justice moved to standardize the collection of suicide statistics across France.[30]

But a lack of evidence did not prevent Guerry's contemporaries from proposing remedies to address the problems he had identified. Indeed, the nostalgic flavor of statistical literature throughout the nineteenth century suggests that anxieties such as Guerry's were not unique and may well have shaped the entire enterprise. In an article that appeared in a medical journal in 1836, the physician M. Brouc traced the increase in suicide, crime, and insanity to the breakdown of traditional social structures and class expectations. Sons disdained the careers of their fathers. Family ties were weaker and offered no consolation when trouble struck, while religion had lost its power over men. "No idea, no external force, no fears for his immortal remains can any longer restrain man from turning against himself that hand given to him for an entirely different purpose," Brouc lamented. Evaluating the data on French suicide for the period from 1836 through 1852, Dr. Egiste Lisle was moved to comment on the profound demoralization produced by the nation's neglect in teaching spiritual values. The statistical increase in suicides, Lisle believed, signified a general indifference to social duties, a fault he did not hesitate to attribute to the materialistic tendency of his age.

The remarkable thing about Lisle's study is that it was awarded a prize in 1856 by the Imperial Academy of Medicine for its scientific merit. Decades later his findings were still being cited as proof of French depravity. "If it is true that the moral poverty of a people is measured by the number of suicides and demented among them," mused one writer in the pages of a statistical journal, "then the figures furnished by the statistics of suicide, at least, are not flattering." Another physician used moral statistics to make a case for social determinism. In times of upheaval, argued Félix Voisin, individuals ceased to belong to the society that surrounded them. Family bonds disintegrated, communities lost coherence, and the social and religious sanctions to which men adhered in stable times no longer held meaning for all members of society. "Being out of harmony with the social order, [the individual] succumbs, according to his nature, to the excitations of the moment," Voisin asserted. "He finds himself battered by contradictory impulses that can make him lose his reason, commit suicide, or go to terrible extremes."[31]

Anyone who is familiar with Durkheim's work on suicide will recognize his famous typologies—the egoistic and the anomic varieties of self-destruction—in the statements of the moral statisticians I have been quoting. Evidence that Durkheim adopted not only the data but also the moral assumptions of earlier writers may be found in the examples he chose to use in illustrating his theory. Egoistic suicide occurred, he claimed, when an individual lost the sense of belonging to his society. Religious beliefs, family responsibilities, and social institutions supplied the *raison d'être* in the lives of most individuals, and when these were undermined, existence itself was threatened. To support this point, he drew an analogy between nineteenth-century France and decadent Rome, comparing the melancholy protagonists of Romantic novels to the suicidal heroes of antiquity. Suicide was "clearly interrelated with the serious disturbances which then afflicted these societies," he wrote. In ancient times, as in his own, it was "the symptom of a morbid condition."[32]

Anomic suicide resulted, on the other hand, from the discrepancy between personal expectations and the actual means of attaining them. In stable times the individual willingly adhered to the standards imposed by his society. "At least if he respects regulations and is docile to collective authority," Durkheim declared, "that is, has a wholesome moral constitution, he feels that it is not well to ask more."[33] But given the tremendous changes the century had witnessed, the political, social, and economic upheavals that began with the French Revolution, he was not surprised that the suicide rate was increasing along with the incidence of insanity, crime, and divorce. While he viewed self-destruction as abnormal and devoted the final chapter of his book to finding a means of diverting "the current of collective sadness" that he identified as its cause,[34] Durkheim chose not to question the "regulations" or to challenge the "collective authority" that produced and maintained such sadness. In this too he seems to have shared his predecessors' assumptions.

Not every nineteenth-century observer was so complacent. French socialists had been employing suicide statistics from the 1830s to point up the government's failure to improve the condition of the majority of its citizens. The so-called moral problems of French society, asserted a columnist in a left-wing newspaper in 1833, might be traced to poverty and the exploitation of workers for the profit of industrialists alone. *Le Populaire*, a journal founded by Etienne Cabet to help spread his utopian communist ideas, printed the following comment at the end of a list of suicide and crime statistics: "And such is the organization of what we call the social order! Such is the society, that knows only too well how to accuse and punish without knowing at all how to prevent and repair!"[35] The fact that the greatest increase in the number of suicides took place among the members of the working class was used by the left to show that poverty did not lead inevitably to revolution or crime. When driven to the end of their resources, these accounts implied, the unfortunate were more likely to destroy themselves than to commit an illegal or criminal act.

By arousing the sympathy of their audience and diminishing the grounds for fear, socialists were trying to persuade readers to shed their excessive concern for self-preservation in order to consider the welfare of their fellow human beings. But the "scientific" analysis pioneered by the moral statisticians and systematized in the sociological method proved far more reassuring in the end. Durkheim's conclusions transformed suicide from a meaningful personal statement into an index of social dysfunction. Personal motivations counted for nothing in his scheme. "They may be said to indicate the individual's weak points," he allowed, "where the outside current bearing the impulse to self-destruction most easily finds introduction. . . ."[36] The subject of the sociological investigation of self-destruction was not the individual but those outside currents that determined human behavior.

Améry reserved his sharpest words for Durkheim, and I now believe I know why. Like the Warsaw ghetto dweller, he felt trapped within the cold enumerations of the statistics, so thoroughly constrained by the language of laws and averages that his independence counted for nothing. The only way of taking back his dignity and regaining his power, of belonging once again to himself, was by deliberately turning his back on the society that had reduced him to a thing. But in abandoning the world he made the point that the world had first abandoned him. Society stands accused by Améry's suicide. "For it and only it caused the disturbance in my existential balance, which I am trying to oppose with an upright gait," he wrote. "It and only it robbed me of my trust in the world."[37]

The most terrible aspect of Améry's suicide, for me, is the harsh vision of reality it affirms. His protest was useless; he knew that. He held no heroic illusions about martyrdom, no dreams of inspiring rebellion through the moral force of his example. Solidarity in suffering was not for him. The brutal logic of the Warsaw Ghetto held true: in a world ruled by violence, it was every man for himself, and fighting back as an individual was the only choice. Améry proclaimed his intent to fight on, to fight to the death, if need be. To the death. His parting word was a line from Schopenhauer. "With death, the world does not change, but stops."[38]

# Death and Democracy

In 1982 a provocative book appeared in France. Written by two veterans of the student demonstrations of May 1968, *Suicide, mode d'emploi* was both a how-to manual and a political manifesto encouraging readers to exercise their right to die. "Half anarchist pamphlet, half cookbook," the Parisian daily *France-Soir* described it in a review.[1] The publication of recipes for self-destruction was something of a cottage industry in the early 1980s. Information about those prescription drugs that would ensure a "gentle death," along with the means of calculating the lethal dose, was in fact derived from earlier handbooks distributed to members of EXIT groups in England and Scotland, the Hemlock Society in the United States, and the Netherlands Voluntary Euthanasia Society.

But the French user's guide was unique. In no other book was suicide endorsed without compunction as a simple expedient to the problems of daily existence. Although organizations promoting voluntary euthanasia operated at that time in most countries of the developed world and in a few third world nations as well, they were devoted to the cause of the terminally ill. "Self-deliverance" for Derek Humphry, author of *Final Exit* and Hemlock's founder, was an option only for those who suffered from painful, incurable physical illness. Indeed, the Hemlock Society specifically excluded from its membership physically healthy but emotionally distraught individuals, advising them to undergo therapy instead of destroying themselves. Only in the French book was the "right to commit suicide" presented as an act of political protest, self-destruction justified as the assertion of personal liberty against "the terrorism of our so-called democratic states." When world leaders justified the proliferation of nuclear weapons as the price of freedom, setting the stage for mass annihilation, suicide might be the only real freedom left: this, at least, was the book's premise. "By affirming the right to die when we choose," the authors exclaimed, "we strike a blow against the thieves of life."[2]

I bought a copy of the book and stayed up late one night to read it. To be honest, I couldn't put it down. The authors' radical credentials, their glee at having wrested the secret of a sure and painless death from the medical establishment, were so tantalizing. Not to mention the recipes. Armed with the information contained in chapter ten, I could walk into the nearest pharmacy and purchase the ingredients for a lethal cocktail. The knowledge both chilled and comforted me. Naturally, I was shocked. The violence of the language, to say nothing of the book's polemical tone, was disturbing to an American unaccustomed to the political tenor of French discourse. To treat

suicide, a subject usually handled with circumspection, so in-
discreetly and so cavalierly, struck me as irresponsible and even
cruel. I couldn't imagine anyone being persuaded by the arguments presented in *Suicide, mode d'emploi*, least of all a person
suffering from a terminal illness, and this made me question the
authors' intentions in undertaking the project in the first place.

In America we prefer to address suicide indirectly. The titles
of the Hemlock Society's two do-it-yourself books illustrate perfectly our culture's uneasiness with the very idea of self-
destruction. *Let Me Die Before I Wake* manages to equate death
with sleep, phrasing the desire to commit suicide as a polite
request, as if to suggest that the potential suicide will await
permission before doing himself in. I could imagine alternative
titles not nearly so reassuring, perhaps: *I Want to Die Now* or *Six
Easy Ways to Kill Yourself.* The best-selling *Final Exit*, subtitled
"The Practicalities of Self-Deliverance and Assisted Suicide for
the Dying," is even more coy. Here, condensed into a single
title, are two euphemisms for suicide—euthanasia as a "final
exit," self-destruction as "self-deliverance"—and a disclaimer
confining the book's audience to people already on the brink of
death. *Final Exit*, as the text on the back cover explains, "is
intended to be read by a mature adult who is suffering from a
terminal illness and is considering the option of rational suicide
if and when suffering becomes unbearable."[3]

Rational suicide. What does this mean? Given the complex-
ity of human behavior, isn't it more realistic to acknowledge
that rational and emotional motivations can and do coexist in
the minds of individuals contemplating self-destruction than to
insist on pure rationality as the grounds for granting the right
to die? I once had the opportunity to ask Derek Humphry this

very question. He was the keynote speaker in a symposium on assisted suicide at the college where I teach, and we were en route to the airport at 6 a.m. the following day. At the podium he'd confined his comments to the situation of the terminally ill: individuals who were in constant pain, had less than six months to live, and were deemed competent to make the decision to die. Under such circumstances, he believed, the right to physician-assisted suicide was fairly straightforward. Of course, physical suffering was one thing; mental anguish opened a Pandora's box of complications that right-to-die activists were understandably reluctant to touch. But wasn't mental anguish a likely product of physical suffering? I persisted. In the privacy of my car on that still-dark morning, Humphry conceded the point.

What I came to realize in the course of our conversation was that his organization was waging a battle on several fronts. Not only were they fighting the religious right, which saw itself as preserving the sanctity of life at all costs. Even those who supported euthanasia in principle needed reassurance that the movement to provide the dying with a sure and painless death would not spiral out of control. The possibility that sick people might be put to death against their will or that healthy people would abuse the information provided in *Final Exit* and kill themselves impulsively could not simply be disregarded.

Most problematic for Humphry and his fellow campaigners were situations where the decision to die was less clear-cut, when subjective considerations pertaining to the quality of life entered into the equation. Many people were uncomfortable with the suicide of Janet Adkins, Dr. Kevorkian's first client, because her action seemed motivated by her distress at the prospect of growing senile and burdening her family, rather than by physical pain and impending death. Adkins had been diagnosed with Alzheimer's but was still in the early stages of the disease when she decided to end her life. "The bulk of health professionals quoted in the media condemned her timing," Humphry noted, "arguing that she had a good deal of quality life still left."[4] Though Adkins appeared competent when she approached Kevorkian, the question being raised here is whether her reason was impaired by her emotional state. Right-to-die activists have resisted such an interpretation of Adkins's behavior, because to allow for the possibility that suicide might be determined by anxiety or depression would strengthen the case for intervention; yet even among euthanasia supporters there is a tendency to defer to authority figures, to keep power away from individuals and place it in the hands of physicians, judges, or legislators. Those who oppose the right to die go one step further, appealing to government or the medical establishment to save us, if need be, from ourselves. Implied in either case is a deep mistrust of the individual and of personal freedom that runs counter to the stated values of our democratic society.

The truth is, we are frightened by suicide. It is painful to imagine that someone we love might choose to die, disturbing to envision the circumstances under which we too might wish to make that choice. Confronted with the suicide of a person we knew, most of us are inclined to seek a psychological explanation for the act. Were they depressed? Did something happen to upset them? Did they show signs of emotional turmoil before taking their life? It is more consoling to regard self-destruction as a passive act than to consider the possibility that someone we cared about wanted to leave us. And it is easier to live with our powerlessness in the face of mental illness than to acknowledge how limited is our capacity to influence the behavior of another human being. Suicide is an affront. Jean-Jacques Rousseau and Alexis de Tocqueville, important theorists of democracy, both understood self-destruction as a threat to communal solidarity. As a political statement, the act denotes dissatisfaction with the present and a repudiation of hope in the future: a negation of the liberal promise on which modern democracies are founded. *Suicide, mode d'emploi* shocked the public because it put the case so bluntly, disregarding the human dimension of self-destruction in order to make a political point, namely, that in trusting our souls to the experts we have surrendered a fundamental right: the ability to determine the manner and timing of our own deaths. "We lose the people we love, we suffer," the authors asserted. "Loss and suffering are the bitter consequences of liberty."[5]

The issue of liberty is clearly at the heart of the euthanasia debate, but whether suicide is a basic right is not as straightforward as advocates would have us believe.[6] Despite the patriotic call of Patrick Henry—give me liberty or give me death—demanding death in a public forum is a sure way of having your freedom curtailed, and for your own good! Henry uttered those stirring words in 1775, in a speech urging his fellow colonists to throw caution to the winds and wage war against the British. An educated man speaking to an educated audience in trying times, he could afford the rhetorical flourish. To threaten suicide as an act of protest against a regime you consider despotic is to invoke the heroic example of Cato, the Roman statesman and defender of the Republic who threw himself on his sword instead of surrendering to Caesar's forces. The good gentlemen of Virginia's Second Revolutionary Convention would not have missed the allusion. Under less dramatic circumstances and in our own times, however, the desire to die appears self-serving and downright un-American. In fact, self-destruction brings out the contradictions inherent in liberal democracy because it represents the absolute exercise of individual freedom, with no regard for personal obligations or community ties.

Our modern notion of democracy emerged out of the eighteenth-century Enlightenment, that moment in the history of Western thought when reason was applied critically to all realms of human endeavor, to social interactions and economic activity, political systems, moral values, and religious belief. Regarding freedom and equality as universal rights—an assumption not held by rulers at the time—philosophers in the cultural capitals of Europe, and in the thirteen colonies as well, challenged those traditional structures that prevented individuals from attaining their potential. Absolute monarchs, established churches, and aristocracies: all would be abolished as free men claimed their God-given right to autonomy. The Declaration of Independence and the United States Constitution both embody this Enlightenment idealism. Our Founding Fathers set out to create a nation whose citizens would be united by fraternity, not fear, a society ruled by justice where equality reigned. Crucial to their vision was a belief in popular sovereignty: the idea that good governments are founded on the consent of the governed. But the thinkers from whom they drew their inspiration disagreed considerably over the ability of men to govern themselves. Democracy was a good idea in principle, but not all were convinced its time had come.

No figure is more representative of the contradictions in

Enlightenment thought than the Swiss writer and political philosopher Jean-Jacques Rousseau. The mistrust of the individual and the appeal to authority figures so evident in the current controversy over the right to die first appeared in his 1761 novel, *The Nouvelle Héloïse*, in its time a cult best-seller.[7] Rousseau's book shaped not only the artistic representation of self-destruction but the terms of the wider moral and political debate over the subject. Following the novel's immense success, other writers were moved to define suicide in Rousseau's terms, as a passionate gesture signifying a crucial failure of self-control, vibrant proof that too much liberty was a dangerous thing. So many of the devices Rousseau employed sound trite to us that it is difficult to appreciate the reactions of his readers, who were encountering them for the first time. The sighs, the swoons, the thwarted love affair, the tormented longing of the hero whose humble origins prevent him from marrying the girl of his dreams, the tragic death of the heroine who expires seconds after affirming her love for her poor but honest suitor: this is the stuff of melodrama, of bad movies and supermarket schlock. To Rousseau's audience, it was heartrending and entirely convincing, so much so that many readers refused to believe that it was a work of fiction.

The story of *The Nouvelle Héloïse* unfolds through a series of letters that pass between the young lovers and their friends and family over a period of years. This format was quite popular in the eighteenth century; the English novelist Samuel Richardson employed it with great success in *Clarissa*, as did Montesquieu in the *Persian Letters*. But Rousseau had an even more famous model in mind as he set out to write his novel. The real-life correspondence of the medieval philosopher Peter Abelard and his student Héloïse had all the elements of a great romance. A brilliant scholar who dared to challenge the reigning ideas of his day, Abelard fell in love with his pupil and married her in secret to give their child a name, but the two paid a terrible price for their impertinence. When Héloïse's uncle learned of the marriage, he had Abelard castrated and forced the pair to take religious orders. The letters they wrote from their respective cloisters are poignant testimony to their enduring love. They never saw each other again.

*The Nouvelle Héloïse* is true to the spirit of the original, but while embellishing the sentimental aspects of the tragedy—the standard edition is composed of six parts, each virtually a novel in its own right, and runs to more than seven hundred pages— Rousseau managed to imbue his version with moral purpose. His young hero, Saint-Preux, is hired by the Baroness d'Etange to tutor her daughter Julie and, like his twelfth-century precursor, quickly succumbs to the girl's charms. The attraction is mutual and overpowering. Rousseau draws out Julie's struggle to uphold her virtue against Saint-Preux's seductive entreaties; the two exchange some forty letters before consummating their union, high-minded expressions of platonic restraint at last giving way to breathless avowals of passionate intensity. Julie conceives her lover's child, but this time it is she who is punished for her transgression. Learning of the affair, the Baron d'Etange beats his daughter senseless, causing her to miscarry, then marries her off to his best friend, Wolmar. The third part of the novel ends with Julie dutifully wedded to a man she does not love while a despondent Saint-Preux, half mad with grief, is sent off on a three-year expedition to the South Pacific by his British friend, Lord Bomston.

Suicide is a recurring motif in Rousseau's novel, but it does not carry the heroic connotations of antiquity. Indeed, Saint-Preux's repeated threats to do away with himself appear petulant and extremely manipulative, not to mention overblown to the modern reader. "The pain you have caused me is without remedy," he tells Julie quite early on, when she is still resisting his advances. "I feel with despair that the fire that consumes me will only be extinguished in the tomb." Stung by her unsympathetic response, he tries another tack: "Order me to die and I will do it." Instead Julie sends him into exile in an unsuccessful attempt to cool his ardor. Addressing her from a remote spot high in the Swiss Alps, his emotional state mirrored in the bleak winter landscape, Saint-Preux imagines that he and Julie might be parted forever. "No, never will I admit that terrible thought into my mind! In an instant, all my tenderness is changed into furor," he writes, comparing himself to a lion, leaping wildly from crag to crag. "I am capable of anything except giving you up," he warns his mistress, "and there is nothing, nothing at all that I wouldn't do to possess you or to die." A few paragraphs later he returns to a description of the landscape in order to underline his point. "I have one more word to say to you, oh Julie!" he exclaims. "You know the ancient use of the rock of Leucadia, the last refuge of so many unhappy lovers. This place resembles it in so many ways. The cliff is steep, the water is deep, and I am in despair." Not even the fulfillment of his desires can keep Saint-Preux's death wish at bay. "Let us die together, my sweet love!" he writes in the morning following their first night together. "Give me the hope of spending a life like this, or allow me to leave one that offers nothing after what I have experienced with you."[8]

Only after Julie's marriage does Saint-Preux contemplate self-destruction in earnest. The most controversial part of Rousseau's novel was not the illicit liaison between the young lovers. It was Saint-Preux's ten-page defense of the individual's right to die when misery overwhelms him: "To seek happiness and flee pain, so long as it does not harm anyone else, is our natural right." A good many readers found Saint-Preux's argument persuasive; Madame de Staël claimed to have been won over by it in her own apology for self-destruction, written some fifty years after *The Nouvelle Héloïse* appeared. But it was hardly Rousseau's intention to make the case for suicide. His final word on the subject was given to Lord Bomston, and it is here that Rousseau first asserted his view of the individual's obligation toward society—a position he would develop in two subsequent works, *The Social Contract* and *Emile*. "If there is still the slightest sentiment of virtue in the bottom of your heart," the English aristocrat admonishes his friend, "come, and I will teach you to appreciate life. Each time you are tempted to quit it, say to yourself, 'let me do one more good deed before I die.' " And he concludes, quite harshly, "If this consideration restrains you from suicide today, it will restrain you again tomorrow; after tomorrow, for the rest of your life. If it does not restrain you, die; you are nothing but a spoiled child."[9]

The moral of Rousseau's story may be summarized in a few sentences: Liberty is a burden only the wise should undertake. The only chance for achieving happiness in this world consists in fulfilling one's duties toward others. Passion is dangerous and ought to be restrained. These lessons are forcefully restated in the second portion of the book. With Julie's marriage, the reader enters the peaceful world of the Wolmar household, a world governed by Aristotelian principles of justice and moderation where order prevails and virtue is achieved through the prudent regulation of passion by reason. Invited to reside within the domestic circle of his former mistress, a chastened Saint-Preux abandons his willful independence and accedes, with a sigh of relief, to his host's authority. "Peace resides in the bottom of my soul, as in the place where I am living," he informs Lord Bomston, ". . . and if I do not have the absolute authority of a master here, I feel greater pleasure in considering myself a child in this house."[10] In this passage Saint-Preux sounds like a wayward adolescent who, after testing the limits of acceptable behavior, has finally found the discipline he was secretly craving. The price of the fleeting happiness he attains, however, is strict self-control. No longer will he indulge in the recklessness of youthful passion. The earthly paradise he finds in the Wolmar household can be sustained only by an effort of will, and if he chooses, upon entering that dreamlike place, to retreat into childhood, we know this condition cannot last. With Julie's death, Saint-Preux will be forced to confront the world in all its misery and imperfection and assume the responsibilities of an adult. And yet, so complete is the transformation in his character that even this tragedy becomes a stimulus to greater virtue. At the end of *The Nouvelle Héloïse*, he is expected to return to her estate and tutor her children, care for her dearest friend, and lead her husband to Christianity. Truly, in the words of the Rousseau scholar Daniel Mornet, "the novel of revolt has become one of resignation and of [the reassertion of] tradition."[11]

Rousseau's concern with his characters' virtue, his stress on social duty over personal fulfillment, and his eagerness to substitute the paternalistic regime of the Wolmar estate for the comparative freedom he allowed in the first half of the novel all attest to his profound distrust of free will and personal independence. Such sentiments seem inconsistent with the democratic ideals he espoused in his political works and his reputed faith in human nature. In fact, this same tension between free will and authority runs through both *The Social Contract* and *Emile*, which is hardly surprising since Rousseau was engaged in writing these books at the same time as *The Nouvelle Héloïse*.[12] By studying the way in which he sought to resolve the problem of liberty in his political works, it becomes clear why his understanding of self-destruction has proved to be so persuasive.

Liberty was the central preoccupation of *The Social Contract*. In the state of nature, Rousseau believed, individuals were ruled by their desires. If there was nothing to prevent them from doing as they pleased, neither were there laws to protect them from the person who sought to satisfy his impulses at their expense. The "natural liberty" found in the state of nature was not true liberty because it permitted the strong to tyrannize the weak. In civil society, on the other hand, individuals were willing to restrict their wants to what they could reasonably have without infringing upon the rights of others. This "civil liberty," while limiting the desires of individuals to a certain extent, assured a greater degree of freedom among the population as a whole. The social harmony that resulted from the voluntary suppression of unruly desires more than compensated for the loss of independence that civil society demanded. "One might also add," Rousseau affirmed, "that in civil society, we gain moral freedom, which is what enables us to become masters over ourselves; for to be motivated by appetite alone is slavery, while obedience to a law one prescribes for oneself is free-dom."[13]

Rousseau's vision of the perfect civil society bore a strong resemblance to the Wolmar regime. There was a familial aspect to his ideal state, with the wise lawgiver taking the place of a father in ordering and shaping the future citizens' lives. The lawgiver's task was not to govern men, however, but to enable them to govern themselves. Like a father, he was preparing his children for the day when they would strike out on their own, using his knowledge of human strengths and weaknesses to erect an invincible structure of rules and institutions that would en-lighten citizens as to their interdependence. Rousseau acknowl-edged that the type of society he envisioned in *The Social Contract* was probably unattainable. "If there were a nation of Gods, it would govern itself democratically," he conceded. "A govern-ment so perfect is not suited to human beings."[14]

Here was the problem our Founding Fathers confronted as they worked to impress democratic institutions upon a popula-tion they did not wholly trust: human nature fell far short of the moral standard their system required. To create citizens capable of exercising their freedom in the disciplined manner they required, one would have to school them in virtue from birth. Such was the project Rousseau undertook in *Emile*: ". . . to give children more real liberty and less power, to let them do more for themselves and ask less of others; so that by teaching them from the start to limit their desires to their ex-pectations, they will not resent the lack of what they cannot have." Once again, it was in learning to tailor their needs to what they could realistically expect to attain that people dis-covered how to be both virtuous and happy. Not only personal satisfaction but survival itself depended upon this ability, for Rousseau anticipated the day when equality would reign throughout Europe and individuals would be forced to rely entirely on their own devices. "We are approaching a crisis, the age of revolutions," he warned, following his dark prediction with a bit of practical advice: it would be wise for even the wealthiest citizen to learn a trade.[15]

Emile is in some ways a pessimistic book, not in the scope of the project it sets forth but in how it accommodates the future. The story ends happily enough, with Emile and his bride awaiting the birth of their first child, whom they pledge to bring up as conscientiously as they themselves were raised. Wanting little more than each other's company, the young lovers live in blissful self-sufficiency, a testimonial to the rightness of Rousseau's teachings. Yet we are aware of how fragile their happiness is. At any moment, circumstances might change. Fortunes vanish overnight. Governments are overthrown. Just men are punished and tyrants rule. With time, even the greatest of passions may fade. Fortunately Emile's education has been designed to see him through any disaster. "It is you, master, who have made me free by teaching me to yield to necessity," the young man assures his tutor. "If it were not for my passions, I should become a man as independent as God himself, since, wanting only what I can have, I would never rebel against fate."[16]

The fairy-tale ending of Emile belies the book's realism. Rousseau was not preparing children to live in a perfect society. On the contrary, his system was devised explicitly to instill the skills they would need to cope with adversity. Nor was it the random blows of fortune he had in mind when he recommended acquiescing to fate. The catastrophe Rousseau feared was nothing less than revolution, with the attendant social and political upheavals all such events entail. To the perils of liberty he enumerated in *The Nouvelle Héloïse* and *The Social Contract* he thus added his misgivings about the progress of social equality. The events that took place in France from 1789 to 1794 seemed to confirm the worst of Rousseau's apprehensions while fulfilling none of his hopes. The essential features of Rousseau's discussion of suicide in *The Nouvelle Héloïse*—his fear of passion, mistrust of liberty, and the value he placed on community—all resonated in the postrevolutionary age. But what seemed to impress readers most was the prescription he offered in *The Social Contract* and *Emile* for creating virtuous citizens in turbulent times: the need to limit one's expectations and adapt to reality.

In the decades following the American and French revolutions, other writers adopted Rousseau's use of suicide as a symbolic means of representing the bounds of individualism within a democratic society. The nineteenth century saw the expansion of popular participation in politics; continuing revolutions in France, reform in England, and the growth of the American republic made it clear that democracy was here to stay. In a democracy, the question of how the masses would deal with freedom became of paramount importance, and the text that proved emblematic in exploring this question was Alexis de Tocqueville's classic study of mass politics in action, *Democracy in America*. Could Europeans learn to govern themselves? Could the people be trusted with power? Observing popular sovereignty in practice, Tocqueville found grounds for optimism about democracy's potential. "The gradual development of the principle of equality is a providential fact," he asserted. Europe was on the threshold of a new era, an era of freedom and boundless opportunity for all members of society. "Gradually the distinctions of rank are done away with; the barriers that once severed mankind are falling," he wrote, "property is divided, power is shared by many, the light of intelligence spreads, and the capacities of all classes tend towards equality." Democracy was proceeding quite independently of any governmental effort to restrain or control it, and so rapid was its progress that no matter how much a nation might wish to return to the hierarchies of the *ancien régime*, it was no longer possible to do so.[17]

Yet Tocqueville's countrymen persisted in their nostalgia for a vanished order, obstinately refusing to confront the challenges of the age at hand. France in the mid-nineteenth century still could not bring itself to embrace the changes wrought by the Revolution. Fearful of moral and political anarchy should the passions of the people again be unleashed, its leaders behaved as if the ideals of 1789 were dead when, in actuality, the desire for freedom and equality now permeated society. As a result, democracy in France had been "abandoned to its wild instincts," Tocqueville complained; "it has grown up like those children who have no parental guidance, who receive their education in the public streets, and who are acquainted only with the vices and wretchedness of society." In his book he returned again and again to the problem of how to reconcile virtue and self-interest within a free nation, echoing Rousseau's insistence on the need to educate citizens in the proper exercise of their independence. Without guidance, democracy threatened to produce a nation of individuals concerned exclusively with themselves. "Thus not only does democracy make every man forget his ancestors, but it hides his descendants and separates his contemporaries from him," Tocqueville warned, "it throws him back forever upon himself alone and threatens in the end to confine him entirely within the solitude of his own heart." The greatest danger democracy posed was to its own survival. A nation comprised of self-interested individuals would not endure. Where Rousseau viewed suicide as a sign of personal irresponsibility, presenting the act in terms of the individual alone, Tocqueville considered it more as a national failing. An entire people might commit collective suicide by refusing to face the challenges posed by the modern world. "Placed in the middle of a rapid stream, we obstinately fix our eyes on the ruins that may still be descried upon the shore we have left," he worried, "while the current hurries us away and drags us backward toward the abyss."[18]

Tocqueville compared France's predicament to the plight of the Indians he encountered on his travels along the American frontier. European portraits of Native Americans during the late eighteenth and early nineteenth centuries tended to emphasize their innate aristocratic bearing, extolling their self-reliance, warrior virtues, and pantheistic reverence for the natural world while romanticizing their "otherness."[19] In Tocqueville's hands, however, these same traits spelled the Indian's doom. Because he preferred to live in the wilderness, the Indian resisted the white man's efforts at improvement, clinging to obsolete ways and traditions out of sheer stubbornness. "Far from desiring to conform his habits to ours, he loves his savage life as the distinguishing mark of his race," Tocqueville contended, "and repels every advance to civilization, less, perhaps, from hatred of it than from a dread of resembling the Europeans." Unlike the poorer inhabitants of Europe, who benefited from their contact with "more civilized" races, as he saw it, ". . . the Indian was indebted to no one but himself; his virtues, his vices, and his prejudices were his own work," he wrote, "he had grown up in the wild independence of his nature."[20]

What Tocqueville termed "wild independence," that combination of pride and freedom leavened with a certain amount of brutality, was the source of the Indian's strength. But the tragedy of the Indians' situation, in his view, lay in the inevitability of their collective self-destruction. "I have passed some time among remnants of tribes, which witness the daily decline of their numbers and of the glory of their own independence; and I have heard these Indians themselves anticipate the impending doom of their race," he noted: ". . . they feel the woes which year after year heaps upon their heads, but they will perish to a man without accepting the cure. Force would have to be employed to compel them to live." Tocqueville recognized that the Indians' predicament was not entirely of their own making. In an angry passage he denounced the United States government for succeeding through perfectly legal, philanthropic, and pacific means in depriving an entire race of its rights and driving it to the brink of extinction. "It is impossible to destroy men with more respect for the laws of humanity," he commented. The Spanish had disgraced themselves in the eyes of the world by the atrocities they committed against the aboriginal population of the lands they conquered, but in the end, they had done a less thorough job than the North Americans.[21]

Still, Tocqueville blamed the Indians for their failure to confront the crisis, to save themselves while time remained. Only by adapting to their changed circumstances, by learning from their oppressors—by following the path Rousseau had mapped out in *Emile* and yielding to necessity—could they hope to survive as a people, yet this they seemed unable or unwilling to do. "The tribes which are in the neighborhood of the whites are too much weakened to offer an effectual resistance," he claimed, "while the others, giving way to that childish carelessness of the morrow which characterizes savage life, wait for the near approach of danger before they prepare to meet it."[22] Tocqueville's Indians were living proof that too much freedom was a dangerous thing. In their stubborn refusal to reap the benefits of civilization, their indolence, pride, and childish disregard for the future, they showed the misfortunes to which an unbridled individualism could lead. As in *The Nouvelle Héloïse*, suicide served as a metaphor for impulsiveness and irresponsibility. There was something terrible in the Indians' situation, a tragedy made all the more inevitable by their apparent unwillingness to assume control of their own fate. Behind the Indians' decision to die rather than give up the smallest bit of their "barbarous independence" was surely rage. How else to explain the tenacity with which they clung to their habits and traditions even when these proved detrimental to their survival? But theirs was an impotent rage, an empty act of defiance that merely furthered the ends of their oppressors. If self-destruction was for them a form of protest against the injustice of white conquest, it was a futile protest that did them no good.

Tocqueville's objective in studying American democracy, as he freely admitted in his Introduction, was to apply its lessons to France: "I confess that in America I saw more than America; I sought there the image of democracy itself, with its inclinations, its character, its prejudices, and its passions, in order to learn what we have to fear or to hope from its progress."[23] His discussion of the Indians fits this agenda but was also part of a larger project, one common to social scientists and literary figures alike during the period when he was writing. From the first voyages of discovery, European explorers were inclined to regard the so-called primitive peoples they encountered as exemplars of human nature in its original state, "noble savages" uncorrupted by civilization. Whereas the Romantics would journey to far-off places in search of self-knowledge, Enlightenment thinkers used travelers' reports of exotic cultures to critique *ancien régime* society and its institutions, projecting their own concerns onto the primitive subjects of their studies. Nineteenth-century anthropologists would continue the practice—even Margaret Mead has been criticized for doing it in her 1930 study of adolescence in New Guinea—and Rousseau's idealization of the state of nature, along with his view of childhood innocence, clearly partakes of the enterprise. So, recognizing that Tocqueville's investigation was shaped by his own preoccupations, what was he really saying about the Indians' refusal to learn from their oppressors?

Tocqueville's diagnosis of the Indians' dilemma epitomized his reservations about the potential for democracy in France, and his greatest apprehension concerned the ability of his countrymen to improve themselves, to correct the deficiencies in their own natures, living neither in the past nor in the moment but with their gaze turned resolutely toward the future. Hope in the future was essential to the success of democracy, Tocqueville maintained, and this was supplied by the Americans' religious faith. In the new republic the spirit of liberty and the spirit of religion were inextricably linked. The Pilgrims' beliefs enabled them to set forth on their journey into the unknown and sustained them through the hardships of their first winter. Civic life in the thirteen colonies was structured around Christian ethics, providing the settlers with an unalterable set of limits within which they could safely exercise their freedom, and this discipline ensured their smooth transition into self-government. Religion also taught them to respect just authority and enabled them to restrain their desires so they could live peacefully with their fellow men: imperatives as vital to Tocqueville's philosophy as they had been to Rousseau's. In fact, this ingredient—religious faith—was grafted onto Rousseau's vision by his famous successor, the Vicomte de Chateaubriand, in an immensely popular tale set in the American wilderness that was surely known to Tocqueville.

In *Atala*, Chateaubriand recast the love story of *The Nouvelle Héloïse* as an American Indian saga.[24] The lovely heroine was the product of a brief liaison between a Spanish missionary and an Indian maiden. Although she never knew her father, Atala was raised as a Christian and had pledged, on her mother's deathbed, to dedicate her virginity to God. The conflicts she subsequently experiences, upon falling in love with the young warrior whose life she saved, drive her to poison herself. "Oh my mother! What have you made me do! Oh religion, at one and the same time the cause of my misery and my joy, my betrayer and my consolation!" Atala cries with her dying breath. "And you, dear and sad object of a passion which consumes me to the point of death," she addresses her beloved, "at last you understand, oh Chactas, the cruelty of our destiny."[25]

Atala's death recalls Julie's in several respects. Each heroine is a passionate creature who despairs of bringing her passion under control, and each expires willingly, secure in the knowl-

edge that she is leaving the world with her virtue intact. Chateaubriand's description of Atala's warring impulses could apply
equally well to Julie: "the spontaneity of her affection and the
purity of her morals, her pride and her profound sensitivity, the
incorruptibility of her soul where great things were concerned
and her susceptibility over small matters . . ." But here the resemblance ends, for Atala's suicide is anything but the passive
act of renunciation that Rousseau's heroine achieved. "At the
very moment that I am to be engulfed by eternity, that I am to
appear before the almighty judge, at the very moment when,
in obedience to my mother, I see with joy my virginity devour
my life," she tells Chactas in the presence of Père Aubry, the
old hermit who has provided a sanctuary for the two lovers,
"by a horrible contradiction, I feel only regret to have never
been yours."[26]

Far from succumbing to death in the approved manner, a
victim of forces she could master in no other way, Atala obstinately destroys herself at just the moment her problems seem
capable of being resolved. "Religion does not demand such a
superhuman sacrifice as yours," the good hermit consoles her,
not realizing his assurances come too late. "Its true sentiments,
its moderate virtues are quite different than the exalted sentiments and the forced virtue of a false heroism." The form of
Christianity Père Aubry represents is nothing like the dogma
Atala had been taught. His is a simple faith that owes more to
inner feelings and the awe inspired by the splendor found in
nature than to the doctrines and rituals of the Catholic church.
Had she but trusted her spiritual instincts, Atala and Chactas
might have lived happily among the small community of Indian
converts the missionary had established in the wilderness. In-

stead she takes advantage of a moment of solitude to consume the poison she has brought from the Indian camp. Atala's suicide is not merely ill-timed. It is senseless and morally wrong, as Père Aubry's gentle admonishments reveal. "My daughter, all your unhappiness stems from ignorance; your savage upbringing and the lack of proper religious instruction have served you ill. You didn't know that a Christian may not dispose of his own life."[27]

The tragedy of Atala's death resonates through the book's epilogue, where the narrator relates his encounter with the surviving members of the tribe to which Chactas belonged. Driven from their ancestral lands by the French, a small band of Natchez is camped near Niagara Falls. The narrator finds them as they are preparing to set out across the Canadian plains in search of a new homeland. Among the sacred possessions they are bringing with them into exile are the remains of Atala and Père Aubry. The old missionary was sadistically tortured and killed, we learn, along with his small flock of Indian converts, by the Cherokees not long after Chactas's departure from the place. But his death was not entirely in vain. "They say that the Cherokees, though accustomed to seeing other savages suffer in silence, could not help but acknowledge that there was something in the humble courage of Père Aubry that was new to them, and which surpassed all earthly courage," a Natchez woman informs the narrator. "Several of them, deeply moved by this death, became Christians."[28]

Through his martyrdom, Père Aubry effects a reconciliation between the Indians and the Europeans. More important, the passive manner in which he dies counteracts the rebellious example of Atala's suicide. The fierce pride of the Cherokees, their bloodthirsty instincts and vengeful spirit, are subdued by the sanctity of their victim's example. Inspired by the supernatural quality of Père Aubry's sacrifice, they embrace the religion of their oppressors. Whether this burgeoning faith will be enough to sustain them through the inevitable territorial losses they face at the hands of white settlers we can only wonder, but it is clear that for Chateaubriand, at least, the consolations of the afterlife were enough to deter the unhappy Christian from destroying himself. At the time he wrote *Atala* he was still living in exile, haunted by the memory of those family members who had perished during the French Revolution. Melancholy reflections on the irretrievability of the past attest to the somberness of the author's mood. Indeed, Chateaubriand's novel is suffused with a sense of loss. "Unfortunate Indians whom I've encountered wandering the wilds of the new world with your ancestors' ashes, you who offered me hospitality despite your misery," the narrator proclaims in the book's final sentence, "I cannot return your kindness because I too roam, at the mercy of men; and less happy in my exile, I have not even brought with me my fathers' bones."[29]

*Atala* ends on an acquiescent note, with the departure of the Natchez on their westward journey. "The next day, at dawn, my hosts bid me farewell. The young warriors led the procession, and the squaws wound it up," the narrator tells us, "the former charged with bearing the sacred relics, the latter carrying their newborn babes; the old trudging along in their midst, placed between their forefathers and their posterity, between memory and hope, between the lands lost and the lands to come."[30] The proud impulse that led Atala to take her life is effectively countered by this closing image. In place of her over-zealous commitment to her parents' faith, we are given the stoic endurance of the Natchez. Like Saint-Preux and Emile, Chateaubriand's Indians learn to accommodate themselves to necessity, patiently bearing their misfortunes and entrusting their lives to fate. Passivity becomes their saving grace, the culmination of bitter experience and a testament to their moral stamina.

Tocqueville's words on the demise of the proud tribes he encountered along the American frontier echo the poignancy of Chateaubriand's closing image. Sympathy for dying Indians was also a key element of the American Romanticism that flourished in the first half of the nineteenth century. Best exemplified in *The Last of the Mohicans*, James Fenimore Cooper's sentimental frontier narrative published in 1826, it also features in the Hudson River School of landscape painting. In Thomas Cole's 1828 canvas *Landscape with Tree Trunks*, the tiny figure of an American Indian warrior can just be discerned alongside the majestic falls. Native Americans also appear in Stanford Robinson Gifford's mid-century painting of Mount Katahdin in Maine, *The Wilderness*, but here they are represented as a vanishing feature of the landscape, "dwarfed by the immensity of the panorama, with perhaps an implication of their impending removal from the place altogether."[31] Of course, the threat they posed in the northeastern United States was minimal by this time; the resistance of the Cheyenne and Sioux was still to come. Yet the menace posed by Atala's suicide is also evident in Tocqueville's treatment of Indians.

Two of the anecdotes Tocqueville provided to shed light on the Indians' character divulge his deeper feelings. The first involves a scene he himself witnessed near a pioneer's cabin in a remote part of Alabama:

While I was in this place (which was in the neighborhood of the Creek territory), an Indian woman appeared, followed by a Negress, and holding by the hand a little white girl of five or six years, whom I took to be the daughter of the pioneer. A sort of barbarous luxury set off the costume of the Indian; rings of metal were hanging from her nostrils and ears, her hair, which was adorned with glass beads, fell loosely upon her shoulders. . . . The Negress was seated on the ground before her mistress, watching her smallest desires and apparently divided between an almost maternal affection for the child and servile fear; while the savage, in the midst of her tenderness, displayed an air of freedom and pride which was almost ferocious. I had approached the group and was contemplating them in silence, but my curiosity was probably displeasing to the Indian woman, for she suddenly rose, pushed the child roughly from her, and, giving me an angry look, plunged into the thicket.[32]

The second anecdote was secondhand, related to him by an American military officer in the summer of 1831:

"I formerly knew a young Indian," said he, "who had been educated at a college in New England, where he had greatly distinguished himself and had acquired the external appearance of a civilized man. When the war broke out between ourselves and the English in 1812, I saw this young man again; he was serving in our army, at the head of the warriors of his tribe; for the Indians were admitted among the ranks of the Americans, on condition only that they would abstain from the horrible practice of scalping their victims. On the evening of the battle of ———, C. came and sat him-

self down by the fire of our bivouac. I asked him what had
been his fortune that day. He related his exploits, and growing warm and animated by his recollection of them, he
concluded by suddenly opening the breast of his coat, saying: 'You must not betray me; see here!' And I actually
beheld," said the major, "between his body and his shirt, the
skin and hair of an English head, still dripping with blood."[33]

The portrait of Native Americans that emerges from these
two stories is not a placid one. The ferociousness of the woman,
her fury at being caught off-guard in a moment of weakness,
the "barbarous luxury" of her attire—and Tocqueville's tone in
describing the beads and nose rings, falling somewhere between
disdain and bemusement: these details serve to undercut his
earlier appreciation for the Indians' dignity. Note the contrast
between the Indian woman's proud independence and the "servile fear of the Negress." Taken together with the bloodthirsty
instincts of the man, which not even a New England college
education could allay, I imagine that many of Tocqueville's readers would have viewed the Indians' unwillingness to "save themselves" with a sigh of relief. Given their ferociousness and pride,
they might easily have chosen to fight back, taking down as many
of their oppressors as possible. Instead they gave up and allowed
themselves to be wiped out. Why should Tocqueville hold this
noble resignation against them?

I see Tocqueville's uneasiness over the Indians' collective
suicide as a reluctant admission of the failure of his cherished
democracy to live up to its promise. The American republic was
founded on hope, after all; liberty meant nothing without the
prospect of a future. In civil society, according to Rousseau,

individuals voluntarily surrendered some of their independence to achieve greater freedom, yet the Indians were made to surrender their independence for the sake of the whites' freedom, not their own. Recognizing that American democracy offered them no future, the Indians chose to die, not, as Tocqueville would have it, out of childishness, sloth, or barbarity but based on an unflinchingly realistic assessment of their chances for survival under white rule.

The terminally ill are in a comparable position, it seems to me. Their adversary—cancer, AIDS, a degenerative disease—is sure to win. Their future prospects are nonexistent. To accept the certainty of your own death is no easy thing, but there are situations without hope. I would say that it requires a great deal of courage to meet this truth head-on, for family and friends no less than for the dying themselves. Our refusal to permit terminally ill people to die painlessly and on their own terms is like Tocqueville asking the Indians to collude in their own destruction. Only here there is no alternative to destruction, which makes our tendency to treat the dying like children all the more deplorable.

# THREE

# Sex and Suicide

He passed at dawn—the death-fire leaped
    From ridge to river-head,
From the Malwa plains to the Abu scars:
And wail upon wail went up to the stars
Behind the grim zenana-bars,
    When they knew that the King was dead.

The dumb priest knelt to tie his mouth
    And robe him for the pyre.
The Boondi Queen beneath us cried:
"See, now, that we die as our mothers died
In the bridal-bed by our master's side!
    Out, women!—to the fire!"

—Rudyard Kipling, "The Last Suttee"

The event depicted in Kipling's poem is startlingly exotic: a Hindu widow, the wife of a Rajput king, prepares to fling herself onto her husband's funeral pyre. "Suttee," remarked the English missionary Edward Thompson in 1923, "reached its most magnificent and least squalid form among the Rajputs"—a strange comment coming from a man intent on exposing the barbarity of the ritual.[1] In fact the Western discussion of widow burning is filled with contradictions, beginning with the very terminology that describes it. *Sati*, the Sanskrit word, refers to the woman whose devotion to her husband is so complete that she is inspired to follow him into death. The Hindu usage emphasizes the conscious intention of the widow and denotes a virtuous sacrifice; shrines are erected to commemorate the *sati*, and the items she has touched are thought to confer blessings on all who receive them. In contrast, the anglicized form, "suttee," refers to the act and, as the words "widow burning" imply, the woman is assumed to be passive, the victim of scheming in-laws or fanatic priests. The language of the British edict that abolished the practice in 1829 reflects this assumption. "Suttee" was explicitly defined by the governor general of Bengal in Regulation XVII as the burning or burying alive of Hindu widows and treated as culpable homicide by the law.[2]

We still think of *sati* as a torment inflicted upon unfortunate women in uncivilized places. "If you had been a British administrator in India," Allan Bloom used to ask his first-year students at the University of Chicago, "would you have let the natives under your governance burn the widow at the funeral of a man who died?" Bloom saw the students' unwillingness to respond to the question with a resounding NO as irrefutable proof that the American educational system had failed them. Who would not condemn the killing of helpless Indian widows?[3] Yet we do say that a woman commits *sati*, in the same way that a person commits suicide, which suggests that the victim immolated herself.

This confusion over just who is responsible for *sati* is not merely a problem of semantics. Sensational accounts of widow burning, particularly during the period of British rule, have shaped our understanding of Indian culture even though the practice was never widespread and is not prescribed by Hindu tradition. Because the incidence of *sati* in the first part of the nineteenth century is known to have increased dramatically in Bengal, the administrative heart of the British empire, both Indian nationalists and modern scholars critical of imperialism interpret the outbreak as a reaction to colonial rule. The idea of *sati* as a protest, an act of resistance to illegitimate authority, also appears in feminist critiques of Indian patriarchy. Given the powerlessness of women in Indian society in general, and the lack of status traditionally afforded to widows in particular, the wife's sacrifice could be read as a stoic reclaiming of self-respect. Even if women were coerced into joining their husbands in death, *sati* stands as an indictment of paternalism, a powerful symbol of the evils of misogyny. And in this regard the European effort to eliminate it in the name of civilization— the humanitarian enterprise memorably characterized by Gayatri Spivak as "white men saving brown women from brown men"— seems suspect.[4]

*Sati* has exerted a powerful hold over the Western imagination. Reading the eyewitness accounts of colonial administrators alongside literary representations of widow burning, I find

not only Bloom's moral outrage but also an unmistakable fascination with every aspect of the ritual. British documents show
that civil servants relished the details far more than their duties
required.[5] Reporting on the 1861 Udaipur suttee following the
death of the last maharana of Rajputana—the same event that
Kipling memorialized—Colonel W. F. Eden, the governor general's agent in the state, described the victim's final moments.
"Mounted on a gorgeously caparisoned horse, herself richly at-
tired as for a festive occasion, literally covered with jewels and
costly ornaments, her hair loose and in disorder, her whole
countenance wild with the excitement of the scene and the
intoxicating effects of the drugs she had swallowed, she issued
forth with the body. . . ."[6] The erotic element of Colonel Eden's
report is even more pronounced in creative renderings of the
ritual. In Goethe's poem, "Der Gott und die Bajadere," the *sati*
was not a virtuous wife but a licentious dancing girl whose
willingness to immolate herself on the pyre of her divine lover
brings about her redemption. Western artists have often portrayed *sati* as an act of passionate abandon, with prostitutes
taking the place of the devoted widows of Hindu tradition.[7] Such
fantasies clearly tell us more about European attitudes toward
women's sexuality than about the Indian culture they purport
to describe. Indeed, the linking of sex and suicide—female suicide—with all the tension this juxtaposition entails, is central
to some of the greatest creations of nineteenth-century art.

Women's potential to disrupt the status quo found symbolic
expression in the adulterous and suicidal woman. Here, embodied in a single compelling image, was everything moralists
feared: the aggressive potential of wives and daughters, as
signified by the unbridled passion that adultery represented; the

bid for power that both adultery and suicide implied; and the coldly rational determination that the decision to kill oneself required, a decision that effectively severed all sense of personal obligation and community ties. Underlying the rhetoric of the male physicians, critics, and social reformers who railed against unconventional women was a terrifying thought: What would happen if the victims in their society stopped being victims and sought revenge for the centuries of oppression they had endured?

The same opposition between virtuous passivity and passionate defiance that emerged in the literature on *sati* comes through in the controversy surrounding *Madame Bovary*, Gustave Flaubert's famous story of adultery and suicide in provincial France. The novel was first published in the *Revue de Paris* in six installments, from October to December of 1846. In January 1857, Flaubert, along with the printer and managing editor of the *Revue*, were brought to trial on the charge of offending public and religious morality. The case for the prosecution centered on the alleged lasciviousness of the novel and its irreverence for the sacraments of the Catholic religion, which Flaubert had described in a language found to be overtly sexual. Emma Bovary's adultery was presented too frankly, without authorial comment upon its impropriety. In lieu of remorse, Emma felt only fatigue as she continued to deceive her husband and neglect her child. And though she died horribly, her suffering rendered in grotesque detail, it was not shame that drove Madame Bovary to poison herself. She never repented her sins.

The court acquitted the three defendants, but not without admonishing the author of *Madame Bovary* that "it is not permitted, under pretext of painting character or local color, to reproduce in all their immorality the exploits and sayings of characters the writer has made it his duty to paint." Flaubert risked corrupting the morals of girls and married women by infusing his prose with sensuality. His realistic style was also criticized for lacking the circumspection of good art. "With him there is no reticence, no veil; he shows nature in all its nudity, in all its coarseness!" maintained the prosecuting attorney, Ernest Pinard. Summing up the affront *Madame Bovary* represented, Pinard claimed that to be virtuous the novel should conform to the highest tenets of Christian morality. "In its name, adultery is stigmatized and condemned not because it is an imprudence that exposes one to disillusionment and to regret, but because it is a crime against the family. You stigmatize and you condemn suicide," he continued, ". . . because it is the contempt for one's duty in the life that is ending and the cry of disbelief in the life that is beginning."[8]

By linking adultery and suicide, Pinard did more than invoke the romantic convention that called for the death of the spurned partner at the end of a love affair. He pointed up the subversive potential of both acts. What led Madame Bovary to commit adultery was her dissatisfaction with the life of a married woman in the provinces—the very life extolled by Rousseau and most reformers at this time. If Charles fails to live up to the ideal set by Wolmar in *The Nouvelle Héloïse*, Emma proves even less suited to the role of Rousseau's heroine. Disgusted with her husband and bored with her child, she possesses neither the wifely submissiveness nor the maternal devotion displayed by the women in the novels she reads.

Emma defies conventions at just those moments when she should conform most faithfully to them. The morning after her wedding night, she behaves like the satisfied husband while

Charles plays the part of the blushing bride. "It was he who could have been taken for the virgin of the night before," Flaubert wrote, "rather than the bride, whose self-control gave no opportunity for conjecture." When Emma does succumb to the attentions of Rodolphe, the closest approximation to a man of the world her small town of Yonville can provide, she does so deliberately, abandoning herself to her fantasies without a twinge of regret, so entitled to romance does she believe herself to be. "She was realizing the long dream of her adolescence, seeing herself as one of those amorous women she had so long envied. Moreover," Flaubert continued, "Emma was feeling a sensation of revenge. Had she not suffered enough?"[9] Such are scarcely the thoughts of a heroine whose moral resistance has been overpowered by the will of her seducer. Madame Bovary's willfulness in fact equals or exceeds the resolution of all the male characters who surround her. Husband, lovers, parents, and priests: none can match her determination.

Emma's defiance of convention is most marked in the affair with Léon. With him she assumes the active role, arranging everything to please herself. In Flaubert's words, "He did not argue about any of her notions; he accepted all her tastes, becoming her mistress rather than she being his." Sexually it is Emma who initiates Léon, she who corrupts and degrades him until at last he turns away in self-disgust. But lust has deprived him of the strength to carry out his resolve. "He resented Emma for this permanent victory over him, even tried not to want her; and then at the sound of her footsteps he felt himself grow weak like an alcoholic at the sight of strong liquor."[10]

This reversal of gender stereotypes was noted by readers at the time. In a review he published in 1857, the poet Charles

Baudelaire drew attention to the androgyny embodied by Flaubert's heroine, who "preserved all the seductiveness of a virile soul within a charming feminine body." Among Madame Bovary's masculine qualities, Baudelaire admired her strong imagination and her vigorous disposition, "that fusion of reason and passion which characterizes men born for action." Beyond this, however, was Emma's immoderate sexual appetite, her desire to dominate her lover, and her vulgar sensuality, all of which merited esteem in Baudelaire's eyes. Madame Bovary's attempt to transcend her petty surroundings, though tragic, was actually the source of her greatness. "Intellectual women should be grateful [to Flaubert] for having elevated the female to such powerful heights, so removed from animal instinct and so close to the ideal man," he effused.[11]

Other commentators were less enthralled by the example set by Flaubert's manly heroine. To Baudelaire's friend and fellow decadent, the critic Jules Barbey D'Aurevilly, Madame Bovary represented "the average woman of declining civilizations, that woman who is, alas! (it makes one tremble) the average woman in societies without beliefs." Emma's immorality was the inevitable consequence of her poorly supervised education. The dreams and ambitions of this "false young lady," the romantic ideals that contrast so painfully with the mediocre reality she is forced to inhabit, thrive in the absence of spiritual guidance. And so when she is invited to the chateau de la Vaubeyssard to sample the life of the declining aristocracy, "the world outside enters in the heart of 'Madame Bovary' never to leave. There it awakens thirsts she will no longer satisfy, even when she slakes them," Barbey disapprovingly remarked. "These men with unknown manners, who have wrinkled her dress while waltzing with her, have infected her with the plague of guilty desires and disgust for the life that she finds again on returning home."[12]

Emma's failing, in other words, is that she has not learned to be content with her lot in life. In a man this might be a spur to greatness, inspiring him to achieve beyond normal expectations. But given the limits placed upon female ambition at this time, the same indulgence hardly applied. Women were expected to find fulfillment in love, confining their talents to the domestic sphere and living through their husbands and sons. A good marriage, a well-managed household, a spotless reputation: in such terms was a woman's success measured.[13] Emma's fall came as no surprise to Barbey, who viewed women as inherently more corrupt, and certainly more dangerous, than men. Death was the best thing that could have happened to Madame Bovary, he asserted, "because if she hadn't poisoned herself on that day, another day she would perhaps have poisoned her husband, like Madame Lafarge."[14]

I find it significant that in his review Barbey chose to invoke the famous French murderess. Marie Lafarge was accused of poisoning her husband in 1840. Her trial and subsequent conviction attracted sensational notice at the time, and her prison memoirs gained her a loyal following, particularly among female readers, for the better part of the nineteenth century. Madame Lafarge's story prefigures Madame Bovary's in several aspects. Married off in the autumn of 1839 to a provincial industrialist who had deceived her family as to his true financial position, she found it impossible to sustain her romantic illusions about married life. "The misfortune of this life is that one dreams about it before living it, and nothing is so sad as being deceived in one's dreams," she lamented during her trial. At first she tried to make the best of her situation, striving to refine her husband's manners and to improve his personal hygiene, redecorating her house according to Parisian standards of taste, even attempting to exert a salutary influence over her husband's employees. But the project must have worn thin in a matter of months, because in January 1840 Charles Lafarge died after a severe intestinal illness, and his wife was indicted for murder.[15]

In depicting Madame Bovary—and virtually every other unhappily married Frenchwoman—as an incipient husband killer, Barbey divulged his real reason for despising Flaubert's fictional creation. The adulteress did not simply undermine the family, that sacred nineteenth-century bourgeois institution. Her crime was more far-reaching, its consequences more devastating than this. Adultery was an act of violence against men and, as such, an expression of woman's rebellious instincts. To clothe these instincts in the language of romance, as if love were all the unfaithful wife sought, was to ignore the seriousness of her transgression. More than a moral failing, adultery was a political act, a quest for power within the confines of the domestic realm that threatened the very structure of society.

Conceding a woman's right to expect love from her husband was the first mistake. In the words of the conservative theorist Louis de Bonald, ". . . it allows the wife, the weaker sex, to rise up against marital authority." Once this citadel was breached, social order would crumble, for in the same way that the husband's authority required the total dependence of his wife and children, the authority of a monarch rested on the absolute obedience of his subjects. The parallels between domestic insubordination and political rebellion could not have been more clearly drawn.[16]

If power, not love, was the driving force behind marital infidelity, women were clearly more dangerous than they appeared. Such a realization may explain the virulence with which some writers attacked adulterous women. Replying in the affirmative to the question, "Should the adulterous wife be killed?" Alexandre Dumas *fils* proceeded to justify his position by arguing that women who refused to accept their subordinate role in marriage were no longer part of divine creation. Akin to beasts, or genetic throwbacks to some primitive state of human existence, they responded to nothing but harsh correction at the first misstep. If punishment didn't work, Dumas *fils* advised the spouse of such a woman, "Declare yourself personally, in the name of your lord, the judge and executioner of this creature. Kill her," he bluntly ordered.

Not even the virtuous wife and mother was entirely blameless in Dumas *fils*'s view, for maternity gave women a kind of moral authority over men which they were inclined to abuse. "She may not regard you as a true husband so much as a *générateur*," he complained, sending you off to work to support her and the children and stifling your own dreams. And since it was she who made the greatest sacrifice in giving birth, she considered your children entirely hers. "Whatever you intended to happen when you encountered woman, it is she who wins," Dumas *fils* warned. "She never takes you for yourself, only for herself."[17]

Granted there were writers who revealed a bad conscience when it came to the question of woman's subjugation in marriage and the implications of upholding the traditional domestic hierarchy for the good of the social order. It was wrong to compare the wife's position to that of a slave, wrote Eugène

Poitou in his prizewinning essay on the influence of literature on public morality. To belittle a woman's proper domain was to invite adultery or something worse. Besides, he bravely went on to assert, "the slave has her empire: the empire of affections in the kingdom of the heart." But though he may have lacked the misogynist fervor of Barbey and Dumas *fils*, Poitou still held the adulterous woman fully accountable for her crime, extending his point to encompass the moral degradation of the poor. Arguing less out of conviction, perhaps, than out of an interest in maintaining the status quo, he warned against the tendency, all too prevalent in modern fiction, to attribute immoral behavior to some uncontrollable instinct, as if fate were to blame for human failings. Similarly, the dispassionate way in which suicide was presented, as a simple alternative to unhappiness, explained why the act had become common. "Ask of life all the pleasures it can provide, and when all the juice has been squeezed from the orange, throw away the rind." Such reasoning only served to relieve individuals of any sense of personal responsibility, encouraging them to believe that if they suffered it was not their fault—encouraging them, in effect, to rebel against whomever or whatever they held to blame for their misfortune.[18]

It was precisely this prospect—that the oppressed members of society might realize their potential to disrupt the established order—that terrified Barbey, Dumas *fils*, and Poitou. Beneath all their bravado was a tacit recognition of the rage behind adultery and suicide. The frustrated wife who took a lover, the impoverished worker who took his own life, were neither inherently evil nor unaccountably perverse. Both were exercising what small amount of freedom they possessed, protesting in the only way they could against the society that colluded in their degradation. Flaubert certainly understood Emma Bovary's dilemma in such terms. "The poetry of the adulterous wife," he observed as he set out to write the novel, "is only true to the extent that she is at liberty in the midst of fatality."[19] But for Barbey, Dumas *fils*, or Poitou to have admitted as much would have been to acknowledge the legitimacy of the wife's or the worker's grievances. Far safer to pretend that those who violated convention were simply immoral than to allow for the possibility that their dissatisfaction was warranted.

The problem was how to do this, how to maintain ignorance regarding the actual motivations for adultery or suicide in the face of everything they knew. At times the ability of male writers to resist the implications of their own arguments was truly astonishing. In a work devoted to proving the proposition that self-destruction was in itself evidence of insanity, Dr. Charles Bourdin found the following case conclusive: A woman who had been unhappily married for several years to a man who abused her, forcing her to work long hours and subjecting her to brutal treatment at home, began to contemplate suicide. For two years she struggled against the temptation, but eventually she succumbed to the impulse to kill herself. "Can this act be explained without recourse to the intervention of insanity?" Bourdin asked. "If it can, then why is suicide not more common among women?" Another physician described the misery of abusive husbands, accepting as a given the prevalence of wife-beating in his society. "There are men who do not cease to mistreat, indeed to beat the woman they love," wrote Alexandre Brierre de Boismont, "and when the victim evades them by fleeing their tyranny, this abandonment is for them a motive for suicide."[20]

In choosing to stress the consequences of domestic violence

while allowing its incidence to pass without comment, Bourdin and Brierre trivialized the experience of abused women in their society. What does it mean, this complacency in the face of female suffering? Both physicians were apparently comfortable seeing women in the role of victim. If Bourdin stopped short of blaming the mistreated wife for killing herself, neither did he evince sympathy for her plight. The fact that she was not stoical enough to bear her pain ad infinitum, as any normal woman would, was enough to damn her. Self-destruction was unthinkable for anyone in her right mind because, by the relentless terms of Bourdin's theory, there was no such thing as a good reason for wanting to die. Well we might wonder that suicide was not more common among women in his day!

Brierre was more accommodating when it came to defining the relationship between suicide and insanity, but the conclusions he drew proved no less disparaging to women. Basing his case on statistics, he claimed that temperamental differences explained why men were three times more likely than women to succeed at destroying themselves. "This numerical inferiority would indicate," he argued, "that to make such a decision requires a degree of energy, of courage, of despair which is not consistent with the weak and delicate constitution of women." Under adverse circumstances, females were prone to go insane rather than take their lives, a tendency he attributed to their emotional instability. Women were sensitive and easily upset, he quoted another physician as saying, but had a horror of blood which, when combined with their flirtatious instincts, made it unlikely they would choose to disfigure themselves in a violent death. They also possessed a stronger family sentiment than men and were more susceptible to religious teachings, "all obstacles which struggle victoriously against the idea of self-destruction." And women were irrational, living by instinct and imagination instead of employing their minds in the logical fashion of men.[21]

Brierre was disinclined to blame a woman for committing suicide because he could not conceive of her making the decision with the conscious determination of a man. In this he diverged from the majority of physicians of his time, who regarded both male and female suicide as the result of insanity. But Brierre's opinion of the weaker sex was consistent with the view of the renowned moral hygienist Alexandre Parent-Duchâtelet, whose 1842 study of prostitution convincingly depicted fallen women as victims driven to practice their immoral profession out of a combination of economic necessity and emotional vulnerability. Prostitutes sinned out of weakness, Parent-Duchâtelet established, they did not set out to do wrong. The majority were genuinely in love with their procurers and remained attached to these men despite the vile treatment they endured. When their poverty and degradation became too much to bear, only a handful attempted suicide. Self-destruction among prostitutes, as within the female population in general, was rare, because even when they wanted to kill themselves, women lacked the guts to carry it out. Though still representing an affront to society, the prostitute deserved to be pitied, not despised.[22]

Of course there was a price to pay for this absolution. The pathetic figures Parent-Duchâtelet and Brierre were creating may not have inspired tirades of disapproval, but somewhere along the way to acquiring their benign status they had also lost their autonomy. Emotionally unstable women were potentially dangerous, but they were easily disarmed. Much like children, they required protection against those who would take advantage of their weakness, and guidance lest they unwittingly harm themselves or another. But under no circumstances should their actions be taken seriously. Their chief virtue lay in their passivity.

The nineteenth-century discourse surrounding women's suicides reveals the same irreconcilable opposition between virtue and licentiousness, submission and subversion that emerged in the treatment of *sati*. I see the joining of adultery and suicide, like the transformation of grieving widows into prostitutes, as a double-edged strategy. On the one hand it served to deprive women of their power to disrupt the established order by denying them any dignity whatsoever. Flaubert's description of Madame Bovary's death is a case in point. After swallowing arsenic, Emma composes a note absolving all around her from blame and prepares for her closing scene. " 'It's really quite simple to die,' she thought, 'I'll fall asleep and it will soon be over.' " A moment later, however, she begins to vomit and experiences excruciating pains in her stomach, preventing her from expiring gracefully as she has planned. The last sound she hears is the crude song of a beggar outside her window. Flaubert even denied her corpse a final glimmer of beauty: "They leaned over to place the wreath on her head. It was necessary to lift the head slightly, and as they did this a stream of black liquid poured out of her mouth as if she were vomiting."[23]

Madame Bovary's punishment was out of proportion to her crime, complained the Romantic poet Alphonse de Lamartine. "Assuredly a woman who defiles the conjugal bed must expect an expiation, but this one is horrible; it is an agony such as one has never seen." But Flaubert claimed that his intention was just this: to incite virtue by revealing the true horror of vice—a

justification not unlike Dumas *fils*'s injunction ("kill her!") regarding the adulterous wife.[24] Such draconian punishment was
the second part of the disarming strategy, the darker part, assuredly, dressed up to look like a moral lesson. Turning Indian
widows into erotic objects was one expression of male fantasies
of subjugation; expiating the sin of adultery by having your
heroine kill herself was another. And there is no better example
of this moralizing zeal than Leo Tolstoy's *Anna Karenina*, the
other famous nineteenth century novel featuring an adulterous
and suicidal heroine.

Anna is certainly more likable than Emma, and far more
complex as a character. Although she is flattered by Vronsky's
attentions, she earns the reader's sympathy by not immediately
giving herself to him. In the beginning of their affair she is
ashamed. Her greatest attribute—the best that can be expected
from any woman, in Tolstoy's view—is her maternal devotion.
She suffers when she is forced to choose between her lover and
her son, but once she and Vronsky are settled in their life
together she seems to grow accustomed to being without the
boy and shows no tenderness at all for their infant daughter. In
a statement that chills her sister-in-law to the bone, Anna makes
it clear that she intends to have no more children. "Why have
I been given reason, if I don't use it so as not to bring unfortunate children into the world?"[25] Cold reason is used by Anna
to deny her womanhood, and as the novel progresses she ex-
hibits other unadmirable traits. She smokes, she drinks, she becomes manipulative, she amuses herself by making men fall in
love with her—arrogant young men or the husband of a former
friend, the pure and decent Levin, it makes no difference. With

these signs of immorality, Tolstoy sets the scene for Anna's suicide.

Anna comes to resent Vronsky for his freedom. Shunned by good society, she is a virtual prisoner in their fancy house, trapped in the role of mistress—a perpetual compromised woman—by her husband's refusal to give her a divorce. Death comes to seem like the only means of escaping this humiliating dependence, but the thought of suicide, of ending her suffering, is mingled with a desire for revenge against her lover for having caused it. "And death presented itself to her clearly and vividly as the only way to restore the love for her in his heart, to punish him and to be victorious in the struggle that the evil spirit lodged in her heart was waging with him." Unhappy, confused, disillusioned with life but, above all, furious with Vronsky, Anna reasons that suicide will bring an end to her troubles. "No, I won't let you torment me," she addresses her absent lover before throwing herself under a train.[26]

Vronsky feels Anna's suicide as a reproach and is devastated by her death. Had it truly been her intention to destroy him, she succeeded admirably. Heading off to martyr himself in the Crimean War, he recalls Anna's final words: "You will regret that," said in their final quarrel. Tolstoy shows us that Vronsky is mortally wounded by Anna's vengeance. "He tried to remember his best moments with her, but those moments were for ever poisoned. He remembered only her triumphant, accomplished threat of totally unnecessary but ineffaceable regret."[27] Here, I think, is the anxiety that fueled Tolstoy's moralizing. Women had more power than they realized; even bad women, like Anna, could wound men by abandoning them, either through death or by withdrawing their love.

I perceive the same fear beneath the misogyny of nineteenth-century physicians. In describing the predicament of men who committed suicide after being abandoned by the women they abused, Brierre showed that males too were volatile creatures ruled by conflicting desires. There is nothing startling in this revelation. The Romantics made a cliché of the angst-ridden hero whose self-destructive despair was inspired, at least in part, by the unattainability of the woman he loved. The emotional sensitivity of men was not at issue in nineteenth-century literature. But where the Romantics were inclined to idealize the female object of desire, Brierre's example presupposes a degree of callousness on the abused woman's part. Without accusing her of intentionally provoking her tormentor's death, he nonetheless made her responsible for the event.

The point is worth emphasizing. For all her remoteness, the Romantic heroine remained a compassionate figure, hovering sublimely just beyond her lover's grasp, powerless to save him but not indifferent to his pain. Julie succumbs to illness rather than violate her marriage vows, victim of a passion she can master in no other way. Only by dying, she explains in a poignant letter to the object of that passion, Saint-Preux, can she allow herself the pleasure of loving him without shame. In a similar fashion, Chateaubriand's Atala poisons herself to preserve her virginity but makes it clear in her final speech that she would have preferred to give in to her lover's entreaties. Both heroines remain virtuous to the end, veritable models of female perfection, but manage to retain a certain vulnerability in spite of their moral fortitude.

Brierre's persecuted woman was another matter. The moment she ceased to be a victim, her tormentor became one, impelled by her courage to take his own life. Ultimately it was she who survived and he who suffered, his misery increasing in direct proportion to her strength. The extent to which suicide implied strength on the part of the oppressed had been Montesquieu's point in the *Persian Letters*, written a century before the works we have been considering. Interestingly enough, a woman's sexual rejection also figures prominently in the book. Roxana, the concubine of a Muslim prince, violates the sanctity of the seraglio first by taking a lover, inciting the other wives to rebellion, and then, when her cause is lost, killing herself in what is clearly a gesture of defiance of her master's authority. "You were surprised not to find me carried away by the ecstasy of love; if you had known me properly you would have found in me all the violence of hate," she taunts him at the book's end.[28]

No one understood the anxiety provoked by strong and sexually independent women as well as the woman writer. Talented and ambitious, she sought a place for herself in the literary domain, a territory reserved chiefly for men where she resided but uncomfortably, an exception tolerated only as long as her achievements did not threaten her male contemporaries. Two women who successfully braved hostility to become legends during the nineteenth century were Germaine de Staël and George Sand. Both authors led unconventional lives and were criticized for immorality. Both were called unfeminine because they demanded to be judged on the same terms as men. And both wrote novels featuring women like themselves, exceptional women who rebelled against social conventions and paid a price for their audacity.

In *Corinne,* Madame de Staël created a heroine at once passionate and rational, dependent and free. Corinne possesses the mental aptitude of a philosopher, the creative genius of a Renaissance artist, and the dramatic presence of an epic hero, yet she also displays the emotional sensitivity and charm of a woman, and a beautiful woman at that. Raised in Italy, her mother's country, she is revered for the superior qualities of mind and soul that set her apart from ordinary mortals, male and female alike. But when she ventures into her father's native England she learns that her gifts are not appreciated. Genius in a woman is too unsettling, and Corinne is not willing to hide her talents for the sake of politeness. "All of paternal authority," as represented by the father of the man she comes to love, condemns Corinne. A marriage is arranged to a man who might have tamed her, "a man so thoroughly convinced of a husband's authority over his wife, and the submissive domestic role of the woman, that the slightest doubt on that score would have revolted him as much as if honor or integrity were at stake." Corinne rejects this match and returns to Italy, where she soon regains her reputation for brilliance. When first glimpsed by the hero, Oswald Lord Nelvil, she is being crowned in Rome for her artistic merit, to the acclaim of the city's entire population.[29]

Unfortunately Corinne's career takes a downhill plunge the moment she and Oswald meet. Captivated at the outset, her lover soon comes to resent her many accomplishments. "He would have liked Corinne to show an Englishwoman's diffident reserve, saving her eloquence and genius for him alone," Madame de Staël notes, stepping out of the story to comment in her own voice: "However distinguished a man may be, the pleasure he takes in a woman's superiority is probably never unalloyed." Pathetically, Corinne tries to dim her radiance for her lover's sake. She puts an end to her public performances. She turns away admirers. She lives only to please Oswald, ignoring the urge to create art for herself. Against Oswald's halfhearted protest that he is the cause of too great a sacrifice, she replies simply, "Talent requires inner independence that true love never allows." Of course, this is a mistake. "For the sake of her happiness," Madame de Staël remarks disapprovingly, "Corinne was wrong to cast her lot with a man who could only thwart her natural self, and repress rather than stimulate her gifts." And ultimately Oswald does the safe (if cowardly) thing, marrying Corinne's younger half-sister Lucile, his father's choice, "the truly English woman who will assure [his] happiness."[30]

In choosing England and Lucile over Corinne and Italy, Oswald feels himself "returning to the life appropriate to men: action directed toward a goal." Italy represented romance to him, but also irrationality and disorder, a frightening combination to a man accustomed to dominating himself and his surroundings. Once back on his native soil, he admires the vigor he sees around him, the signs of industry and prosperity that characterize the well-ordered kingdom that is his home. "Reverie," he convinces himself, thinking of Corinne's country, "is the portion of women, of beings weak and submissive from the day of their birth." So it is that virile England defeats passive Italy, masculine reason vanquishes feminine passion, and conventionality triumphs.[31]

Or so it seems, at the point in the novel when Oswald weds Lucile and Corinne returns, grieving and close to death, from an ill-advised trip to England to see him. But Madame de Staël did not end the novel there. Instead we follow the characters through three more chapters spanning four years in their lives.

In that time Oswald is made to suffer, the cruelty he showed in turning his back on Corinne troubling his conscience and blighting the happiness he expected to find in marriage. Lucile suffers too. Newly married, she is abandoned almost immediately when Oswald's regiment is called to fight against the French Revolution. During his lengthy absence, she comes to learn all the details of his relationship with Corinne, and after this nothing is the same between them. For the sake of Oswald's health, the couple travel to Italy with their three-year-old daughter Juliette, who bears a striking if unlikely resemblance to Corinne. They arrive in Florence to find Corinne at death's door. Devastated by Oswald's betrayal, she has been unable to recover either her talent or her health. Indeed, from the moment she released him to marry her sister, she has wanted nothing more than to die. At last, in the presence of her repentant ex-lover, she gets her wish.

No less than for Anna or Roxana, death is a weapon for Corinne. At the first hint of trouble, she threatens to die. "Be free then, Oswald, now and every day, free even if you were my husband," she writes when he balks at the idea of marrying her against his dead father's wishes, "for if you no longer loved me, I would free you by my death of the indissoluble ties that bound you to me." In the end, Corinne has her revenge. What is more, she obtains it blamelessly, virtuously even, expiring of illness in classic feminine form. Corinne's fatal illness is never named. Its symptoms resemble those of consumption—fever, faintness, unnatural bursts of energy followed by longer periods of lethargy—but we know better. Madame de Staël's heroine dies for love. Unlike the traditional lovelorn female, however, stock figure in the Romantic literature created by men, Corinne's exit is anything but acquiescent. She may not have died by her own hand, but it is apparent that Corinne has willed her death, and willed it in such a way as to cause Oswald pain. After she is gone, Oswald falls into a frenzy of remorse. "He was so wild that at first they feared for his reason and his life." Eventually he settles down and resumes his ordered existence, but Madame de Staël is not content to leave him there. "What became of Oswald?" she asks in the book's final paragraph. "Was he consoled by society's approval? Was he satisfied with an ordinary lot after what he had lost?" Hopefully he was not, though the author refrains from saying so outright. "I do not know," she concludes coyly, "and on this score I wish neither to blame him nor to grant him absolution."[32]

Corinne's death packs the punch of suicide, yet Madame de Staël's character manages to remain sympathetic despite the injury she inflicts. She does this by veiling her anger, channeling it into illness, and clinging to the role of victim to the bitter end. Nowhere does she protest against the injustice of her position: an extraordinary woman consigned to a life alone because she cannot conform to men's expectations. Madame de Staël's readers were left to draw the conclusion for themselves.

Rage is much closer to the surface in *Lélia*, George Sand's self-confessed autobiographical novel of female frustration. From the outset its heroine displays a dangerous independence. Lélia demands the rights of a man in her society, the freedom to confer her sexual favors as she pleases, to exercise her intellect, and to achieve prominence on her own. Compared to Shakespeare's tragic heroes Hamlet and Romeo, to Juliet, "half-dead and concealing in her breast the poison and the memory of a shattered love," and, tellingly, to Corinne, Lélia stands apart from these figures on account of her emotional coldness. This coldness is central to her character and seems part of her allure, but it proves to be her undoing.[33]

The menace implied in Lélia's remoteness, the power it confers, is half perceived by Sténio, the young poet who loves her. "Watching her come toward him, alone and pensive," Sand writes, "he felt something like hatred for this creature who was held by no apparent bond to nature." If Lélia were a true woman, presumably she would have succumbed to nature and returned the poet's love. But Lélia is incapable of love. At times she almost regrets this, such as when she exclaims, at the tomb of a woman who died of a broken heart, "To live and die for love! How beautiful for a woman!" But elsewhere she expresses an unwillingness to efface her existence in this way. "Oh, I remember the burning nights I passed pressed against a man's flanks in close embrace with him," she confesses. "During those nights I thoroughly studied the revolts of pride against abnegation. I sensed one could simultaneously love a man to the point of submitting to him and love oneself to the point of hating him because he subjugates us."[34]

The destructive side of love, the risks it holds for lover and beloved alike, are repeatedly stressed in Sand's novel. Sténio cannot live without Lélia; more than once, he attempts suicide to punish her for her indifference. "Now I renounce love, I renounce life: are you happy? Adieu!" he threatens early in the novel. And in the book's penultimate chapter, he makes good on his threat and drowns himself, reviling Lélia with his dying breath. What Sténio wants is only what every man wants from a woman. Putting it bluntly, Sand has him say, "Is it not the essence of man to want to possess what he admires? When you come upon a beautiful flower, don't you want to breathe its perfume, hide it in your breast, pull it out by the roots in order to have it all for yourself, for yourself alone?" Rather than allow herself to be possessed in this way, Lélia chooses to remain detached and alone. She is not even willing to submit herself to God. "I would be an adulterous bride for Christ," she announces, when asked why she has not renounced the world since she despises it so much, and become a nun.[35]

Love and faith, the traditional outlets for women at this time, hold no appeal for Lélia because they make women passive. Even suicide strikes her as a kind of defeat. It is an act "more cowardly," she claims, "than enduring this defiled life God, in his contempt, has left to us." Yet in the end she is made to become a victim in spite of herself. Magnus, a priest driven mad by his love for Lélia, rails against God for allowing him to suffer the pain of an unrequited passion. Only when Lélia is dead, he believes, can he regain his faith and tranquility, and so he strangles her, crying, "When you are dead, I will fear you no more! I'll forget you and I'll be able to pray." The novel concludes with this irony, that Lélia should die not by choice but for the sake of love and religion, forced to resume a traditional role. Here was Sand's bitter comment regarding the fate of strong and sexually independent women in her society.[36]

Sex and suicide, love and death: the most striking and enduring expression of the dangerous tension between our creative and destructive urges is Brünnhild's joyful self-immolation at the end of Wagner's *Götterdämmerung*, the final opera in his famous *Ring* cycle. Brünnhild is no typical *sati*. A warrior goddess, she possesses a terrifying power. In love or in anger, she is a force to be reckoned with; she alone holds the ring of gold that gives its owner absolute dominion over all other creatures. But Brünnhild renounces her power for love, freely choosing to throw herself, along with the ring, into her husband Siegfried's funeral pyre:

> Grane, my horse!
> We meet once more!
> Do you know, my friend,
> Just where we are faring?
> In radiant fires
> There lies your lord,
> Siegfried, the lord of my life.
> You're joyfully neighing
> Just to be with him?
> Laughter of flames
> Allures you to follow?
> Feel how my bosom
> So hotly burns.
> Radiant fire
> Takes hold of my heart.
> On to embrace him,
> To live in his arms,
> Thus yoked to him ever
> In mightiest love![37]

All the paradoxes revealed by the nineteenth-century discourse surrounding women's suicides are somehow resolved in Brünnhild's final oration. Hers is a virtuous sacrifice that is also willful and passionate, a renunciation that is also an embrace. An act of supreme vengeance that is also a supreme act of love. Wagner conceived the *Ring* cycle as a political parable. Living in exile in Zurich after the failure of the 1848 revolutions, he wrote the sketch that would later become the *Götterdämmerung* in a pessimistic frame of mind. Only the complete destruction of Western civilization would bring about the freedom he craved. "After the fullest sober consideration, and with my feet firmly on the ground," he wrote to a friend in October 1850, "I assure you that I no longer have faith in any revolution unless it begins with the destruction of Paris by fire."[38] Yet there was hope at the end of the opera: a new order would be created out of Brünnhild's suicide. The *sati*'s death, her willing sacrifice for love, would confer a blessing after all.

Wagner achieved the impossible. Through art he found a safe means of conveying his rebellious message, containing the threat posed by the suicide of the oppressed while allowing his political passions free reign. If literary representations of adulterous and suicidal women served to express anxieties or, in the case of women writers, frustration over the victim's place in society, such images could also incite public hostility, as the critical reception of *Madame Bovary* clearly demonstrates. But in the *Götterdämmerung*, art became the means of creating an imaginative realm where unruly desires could be expressed without risk. Wagner's ability to impose his vision on the world raises an intriguing possibility—one already anticipated by Flaubert in his parody of Emma's attempt to live her life according to the conventions of Romantic fiction and, when all else failed, to die beautifully. Suicide could be a creative act, a final effort at self-expression made with an audience in mind.

# FOUR

# Leaving You

H<small>E WAS</small> already a cliché in 1831 when Balzac satirized him
in the *Peau de chagrin*: the sensitive young man who kills himself
in despair when the girl of his dreams rejects him, the angst-
ridden artist whose brilliance is appreciated too late, alas, by an
unfeeling world. On the verge of putting an end to his tiresome
existence, Raphael Valentin, the hero of Balzac's novel, consults
his worldly friend Rastignac on the most aesthetically correct
means of committing suicide:

> "What do you think of opium?"
> "Oh no! Extremely painful!" Rastignac replied.
> "Charcoal fumes?"
> "Too vulgar!"
> "The Seine?"
> "The drag-nets and the morgue are very filthy."

"A pistol shot?"

"Suppose you miss? You're disfigured for life."

What appeals most to Valentin's delicate sensibility is Rastignac's final argument: "Tradesmen have brought the river into disrepute by throwing themselves in so as to soften their creditors' hearts. If I were you, I would try to die elegantly." Listening to his friend, Balzac's character is persuaded to destroy himself aristocratically, by overindulging in pleasures. "Intemperance, my boy, is the most royal of deaths. It has lightning apoplexy at its command. Apoplexy is the pistol-shot that does not miss," Rastignac assures the reluctant Valentin. In contrast to "the swollen bellies and the decomposing green and blue flesh" of the morgue, the two can enjoy orgies and gambling, prostitutes and wine: a more enjoyable way to go, without a doubt, but one hardly in keeping with the Romantic temperament.[1]

A longing for death was a sign of sensitivity and creative promise among early nineteenth-century artists and intellectuals. "Suicide," noted the influential critic Saint-Marc Girardin in 1843, "is not the malady of one who is simple of heart or mind; it is the malady of the refined and of philosophers."[2] Alphonse de Lamartine, George Sand, Alfred de Musset, Germaine de Staël, Benjamin Constant, and the Vicomte de Chateaubriand all confessed to having been tempted to kill themselves in their youth, but each was moved, in later life, to repudiate the desire. So it was that Chateaubriand narrated the story of his adolescent attempt at self-destruction. When despair pushed him to the brink of suicide, fate stepped in to thwart his plans: "I assumed that my final hour had not yet come, and I put aside until another day the execution of my project." After all, had he succeeded in terminating his life, he explained with characteristic immodesty, "people would have known nothing of the story that nearly drove me to a catastrophic end; I would have swollen the ranks of the nameless unfortunates."[3] Those who pursued oblivion too aggressively, seeking out death as opposed to allowing it to find them, ran the risk of losing the sympathy of their audience.

Rastignac's advice to the contrary, posthumous reputations were enhanced by suffering. The tragic figures in Romantic fiction generally succumbed to accidents or illness, languishing for several pages, and sometimes chapters, before quietly expiring offstage. René and Raphaël, the title characters of Chateaubriand's and Lamartine's famous novels, found comfort in contemplating their unhappiness, nourishing their despair and painfully reliving the past, devoting themselves so completely to sustaining their sorrow that they soon forgot there was any other way to live. Thus René describes his remorse upon realizing it was his sister's forbidden love for him that drove her into a convent: "I derived an unexpected kind of satisfaction from the experience of grieving, and I realized, in secret joy, that pain is not as easily exhausted as pleasure. . . . And strangely enough," he continues a paragraph later, "I no longer wished to die since I had become truly unhappy. My grief became an occupation that filled all my waking moments." Raphaël finds a similar satisfaction in savoring his depression. "I plunged myself into the abyss of sadness," he writes in his journal. "An illness, without a doubt, but an illness whose actual texture is seductive rather than painful, wherein death comes to seem like a voluptuous surrender into infinity."[4]

The nineteenth-century infatuation with dying was not confined to the literary realm. Ordinary men and women endeavored to stage their own closing scenes, adapting the Romantic script to fit their circumstances. And why not? According to the cultural conventions of the period, a good death could redeem the least sympathetic character. In a scene in Victor Hugo's *Les Misérables*, Inspector Javert, having allowed the presumed criminal Jean Valjean to escape, contemplates the ethical implications of his spontaneous act of mercy. "Was there anything in the world except courts of law and death sentences, authority and the police?" Hugo's character asks himself. "He felt as if he had been torn out by the roots. The law he lived by was crumbling to dust in his hands. . . ." Unable to resolve the contradictions between the laws of society and the promptings of his own conscience, Javert determines to drown himself in the Seine. In the context of the novel, this final decision bestows nobility upon the inspector, providing him with the humanity he lacked in the preceding thousand pages. Elsewhere in *Les Misérables*, however, Hugo displays a less favorable attitude toward suicide. Faced with an equally serious dilemma, his main protagonist never considers taking his life. "Suicide, that mysterious assault upon the unknown, which might even entail the death of the soul, was impossible for Jean Valjean."

Where Javert can conceive of no alternative to suicide when the grounds for his certainty are shattered, Valjean is preserved from the same temptation on countless occasions by his love for the child Cosette and by the strength of his spiritual beliefs. Valjean's religious convictions, his abstract, almost deistic faith, are central to his character as Hugo imagined it. Virtuous to a fault, he once takes part in a revolutionary battle and emerges unscathed from the fighting. Though he takes great risks in rescuing the wounded from the barricades, "he did not fight or strike the slightest blow, even in self-defense." What motivates him in his selflessness and courage, Hugo is careful to point out, is not an instinct for self-annihilation. "If suicide had been his intention when he went into that tomb, in this he had failed completely. But we doubt whether he was contemplating suicide, an irreligious act."[5]

The distinction Hugo draws, between Valjean's principled refusal to act on his self-destructive impulses and Javert's troubled plunge into the abyss, is an important one because it points up the contradiction inherent in the Romantic depiction of suicide. The greatest heroes did not presume to undo their destinies; they found solace in enduring their sorrow with quiet dignity. Sténio drowns himself when he realizes that he will never fulfill his creative promise or attain Lélia's love. His death is foreshadowed at several points in the novel, always in disparaging terms. "Young man, you are able to endure suffering," Lélia admonishes him at one point, "and yet you talk of suicide, which is more cowardly than undergoing this defiled life God's contempt leaves us." In Sand's vision, as in Hugo's, suicide was the last refuge of weaker souls. But when Sténio's suffering finally drives him to renounce his existence, his end is portrayed compassionately, and Sand goes so far as to suggest that he has achieved through his death the perfection he failed to attain in life. Bedecked with flowers and aromatic herbs by the mountain peasants, the poet's corpse receives the love Lélia had denied him when he was alive. "You did well to die, Sténio. Your great soul was suffocating in this delicate, frail body and in this sunless world," she addresses the lifeless body. "I go on my knees to tell you that I love you, now that you seem deaf to my avowals and insensitive to my caresses."[6]

Readers absorbed these lessons as they attempted to write their own grand finales. Success hinged on your ability to portray yourself as the victim of injustice or of a cruel and inexorable fate. Emotional turmoil strong enough to distort your judgment also counted, provided you still preserved a vestige of rationality—enough to suggest that you were aware of the dangerousness of your situation while still demonstrating your inability to master it in any way short of suicide. For people feeling neglected or misunderstood, the opportunity to create, through death, a final statement that would imbue not only their last moments but their entire life with significance proved irresistible. But Romantic formulas served to obscure the purposeful aspect of self-destruction. The last remark is the right one, quipped Roland Barthes in *A Lover's Discourse*, his critical exploration of the genre. "To speak last, 'to conclude,' is to assign a destiny to everything that has been said, is to master, to possess, to absolve, to bludgeon meaning. . . ."[7] The trick lay in controlling how that last remark would be interpreted.

Included within the police records in the French National Archives are the results of local investigations into suicides and accidental deaths for every *département* of France during the period 1815–1830. Whatever light could be shed on the circumstances surrounding a suspicious death, either through the testimony of witnesses to the event or by persons close to the deceased, and whatever traces the individual left behind that might furnish a motive for suicide—unpaid bills, lottery ticket stubs, correspondence, and the occasional suicide note—were dutifully described in the prefect's report in support of his judgment regarding the voluntary or accidental nature of the death under investigation. Reading these documents, which span the era when Romanticism flourished, I came to appreciate the allure of the literary conventions surrounding self-destruction: the sentiments expressed in one report after another bore the unmistakable imprint of the Romantic spirit.

In the spring of 1826 a young pharmacist's assistant in the Hautes Pyrenées wrote the following words to his guardian:

> It is Sellier who traces the last lines that he truly will ever write to you. I am going to die, Monsieur Laffourcade. That is a fact. In a few hours, this hand that writes to you will be cold and lifeless; already the pallor of death is visible on my face, my features already show signs of the crime that I am about to commit. But Adila Gaillard has too grievously wounded my heart, for me to heed the call of that virtue to which I never seriously subscribed. . . .

What was I to make of this statement, and of the testament Sellier also found the time to write bidding the world and "cruel Adila" adieu, and leaving her half his fortune "if she would deign to accept it from these blood-covered hands?" It would appear that Sellier wished to cast himself in the role of tragic hero in a drama of unrequited love, a common enough scenario within the artistic discourse of the time. That he may have overdone the pathos by actually shooting himself beneath Adila's bedroom windows "so that she may be the first to hear the pistol shot when I blow my brains out," as he put it, only slightly mars the impression he sought to create.[8]

For Sellier's gesture to have been effective, of course, the participation of Adila and Monsieur Laffourcade was required.

Only if they recognized his literary allusions would his death be interpreted sympathetically, not as the hostile act of retribution that I discerned beneath the poetic language but as the last recourse of a tormented soul. In this case the plot was borrowed from a highbrow source: the semi-autobiographical novel of Johann Wolfgang von Goethe, the father of German Romanticism. *The Sorrows of Young Werther* inspired scores of copycat suicides across Europe following its publication in 1774, so many that Goethe was driven to caution readers, in the epigraph to the second edition, against taking his message to heart: "Be a man, he said; do not follow my example." The book was instantly translated into French and English; Napoleon Bonaparte claimed to have read it seven times, and it was among the topics he and Goethe discussed when the two met in 1808 at Erfurt.[9]

Werther's story is certainly compelling. An artistic young man takes himself to a small town in the German countryside where he hopes to regain his equilibrium. There is a suggestion that he has misled a girl into thinking he loved her, and that he in turn loved another, older woman whose death he is mourning. He finds comfort in the beautiful surroundings and in the simple peasants he encounters on his solitary walks, but soon he meets the woman who will alter his destiny. Lotte is a charming creature who shares his sensitive disposition and his love of medieval romance. Unfortunately she is engaged to a man named Albert; it was her mother's dying wish that the two should marry, and Lotte is nothing if not a dutiful daughter. She offers Werther the consolation of a three-way friendship, but he, naturally enough, finds this arrangement intolerable. He cannot bear to see Lotte and Albert together, yet he cannot bear to live apart from his beloved. Following their marriage, he resolves to kill himself. "One of us three must go," he writes to Lotte on the morning of the day he plans to die. "When you read this, my dear, a cool grave will already be covering the rigid remains of the unfortunate who knows no greater sweetness to fill the last moments of his life than to converse with you." A few hours after penning the note, he shoots himself with one of Albert's pistols. "Oh, that you two might be made happy by my death!" he tells them in his closing lines. "Lotte! Lotte! Farewell! Farewell!"[10]

The parallels between the plot of Goethe's novel and the fate of the young pharmacist Sellier are too close to be coincidental. Perhaps those moralists who blamed the Romantics for inciting suicide had a point. German pastors condemned the book when it appeared, and *Werther* was actually banned in some countries. In the decades following its publication, copies of the book were found tucked in the jacket pockets or lying open on the bedside tables of unhappy lovers who took poison, shot themselves, leaped to their deaths, or drowned. By the middle of the nineteenth century, Goethe's book was still being held up as an example of irresponsible authorship. Writing in 1855, Henri Blanchard proposed that the Académie Française award a prize to the drama that presented suicide in the least favorable light. Works such as *Werther* should be satirized, he maintained, and if this did not suffice to deter people from following the hero's example, the names of each suicide should be published in the newspaper succeeded by the words: "Suicide, coward, deserter of the sacred duties of man and citizen." Saint-Marc Girardin also found little to admire in the self-destructive heroes of Romantic convention. Whereas classical French dramatists had portrayed suicide as an act of desperation, modern theatre, in his view, seemed to ennoble it. "And here it is not theatre that borrows its ideas and passions from society," he lamented, "it's society that sadly imitates theatre." A professor of literature referred to these arguments in 1910 when making his own case against the corrupting influence of the novel. By reading the diaries and correspondence of ordinary people during the period when Romanticism flourished, Louis Maigron claimed to have discovered how the Romantic "taste for the bizarre" filtered down to the masses, producing among the young especially that fatal *mal du siècle*, suicide. "A fevered and morbid exaltation, the weakening and then the ruin of the will: that is Romanticism," he charged.[11]

Did the artistic veneration of suicide in the first decades of the nineteenth century really influence susceptible souls like Sellier to take their own lives? My research into the cultural conventions surrounding self-destruction at this time suggests a more complicated interaction than the moralists wished to acknowledge—less a case of life imitating art, in fact, than of life superseding art: reality doing art one better—a tendency that Balzac also shrewdly dissected in *La Peau de chagrin*. "Where will you find, emerging from the ocean of literature," he asked, "a book that can vie in genius with a news-item such as: *Yesterday, at four o'clock, a young woman threw herself into the Seine from the Pont des Arts*."[12] Romantic formulas clearly offered some individuals a culturally sanctioned means of acting out their frustrations; but this is not to say that suicide would not have existed without such a vehicle for self-expression, or that the feelings that really drove people to seek their deaths necessarily coincided with the sentiments they chose to exhibit in suicide notes. Rather, these formulas provided people with a language in which to express their unhappiness, a set of symbols and associations that would be understood by other members of their society. The individuals I encountered in nineteenth-century suicide notes, like the Romantic artists whose works they so obviously admired, were engaged in a creative enterprise. Contradictory as it may sound, they sought to construct their identities through the act of destroying themselves.

The composition of *Werther* illustrates perfectly the creative interaction between art and life. At the time he wrote the novel, Goethe himself was in love with a young woman named Charlotte (Lotte) Buff, who was engaged to marry his friend, the diplomat Johann Christian Kestner—not that this was his first unrequited passion, but the sorrows of young Werther are known to have mirrored Goethe's own suffering at this time. More than once, Goethe told his audience, he came close to committing suicide on account of Charlotte Buff; a good number of the letters that comprise the novel were little more than word-for-word renditions, in fact, of the correspondence that passed between the author and his friends at the time. While still a student, Goethe had expressed a desire to "contrive his life as a novel," to live each day as if he were a character in a book, and so it should come as no surprise that his personal story of frustrated desire also bears an uncanny resemblance to another literary work with which the German author was undoubtedly familiar: the *Nouvelle Héloïse* of Jean-Jacques Rousseau. Written in 1761—eleven years before the events that inspired Goethe's own drama—the novel had seventy-two printings in the first forty years following its publication. Napoleon kept a copy of this book, too, in his library.

Two years before *Werther* appeared, another acquaintance of

Goethe's, Karl Wilhelm Jerusalem, had shot himself with a pistol he'd borrowed from Kestner. *Emilia Galotti*, a tragedy by Gotthold Lessing, was found lying open beside the young man's body. The same book sits open on the desk where Werther writes his final letter to Lotte. As in the case of Sellier, I want to question Goethe's motives in publishing *Werther*, which was not only his story, after all. It was also Charlotte Buff's story, and the story of his friend and rival Kestner. What was their reaction upon reading the book and witnessing its extraordinarily successful career? For decades following the novel's publication, a steady stream of pilgrims showed up on Buff's doorstep, all eager to meet the real-life inspiration for Werther's true love. For his part, Kestner complained that Goethe had hardly done him justice in the character of Albert. The beauty of *Werther*, and the actual suffering known to have inspired it, distracts the reader from the darker impulse behind the book's creation, namely, the author's desire to injure Buff and avenge himself against Kestner. Indeed, Goethe warned the couple in a letter that he was intending to write about them: "And if it should enter your heads to be jealous, I reserve the right to present you on the stage, and with the most telling strokes!"[13]

I seem to be caught in a circular argument. Goethe's novel helped shape the Romantic image of suicide, providing troubled souls such as Sellier with a ready-made script they could adapt for their own purposes. This script, as it turns out, was not original. Goethe borrowed the plot from the real-life suicide of his friend, and both Goethe and the unfortunate Jerusalem wrote their stories in the language of Rousseau. Given the extent of the borrowing, to what degree were the feelings expressed by any of these people genuine? I do not mean to suggest that Goethe did not love Buff or that Sellier was not hurt by Adila's rejection, but the ways in which each of these men *experienced* their love and their pain were clearly shaped by convention. The Romantic script governed not merely the form in which feelings were conveyed to others; the language of Rousseau and his imitators, both great and small, set the terms by which nineteenth-century men and women interpreted their own experiences. This same language also enabled them to conceal less-than-noble impulses behind a veil of sentiment, to deceive not only the world but also themselves as to their true motivations.

In 1816 a thirty-three-year-old man from the Gironde shot himself, ten days after his wife left him. Neighbors attested that he had mistreated her for many years, but in a note found in his pocket he staunchly asserted his blamelessness: "Since I have always been misunderstood, I'm telling you that these pistols are only for my own destruction. God alone knows my soul, my innocence and my virtues." In 1825, Noel Delamotte's rotting corpse was found in the Ardennes woods. The young man had gotten the notary's daughter pregnant and shot himself to avoid marrying her. This, at least, was what townspeople surmised. "Life has become a burden for me," was all he chose to reveal of his motivations. In 1820 the former director of the Etain post office in the Meuse was found shot. In his note he claimed to be an honest, God-fearing man who was reduced to despair by the "infamous conduct" of his denunciators. "I have no choice but to end my days as the pure victim of their sinfulness," he exclaimed, adding politely that he had no need of a religious funeral but hoped to be remembered kindly by those who knew him. In 1816 the thirty-nine-year-old wife of a dye worker in Amiens, a woman known to have a drinking problem, threw herself in the river. "Kiss my children for me," she instructed her husband in the letter she left behind. "I am leaving Amiens. *Adieu pour la vie* [Goodbye to life forever]."[14]

The readiness with which nineteenth-century men and women resorted to the Romantic script when contemplating their own destruction is an indication that the language of Rousseau and Goethe had permeated European society. How widespread was this tendency? Did anyone weep over the real-life suicides the Romantics supposedly inspired? In the case of Sellier and the individuals I have just described, the reaction of those affected by the deaths is not known, and the prefects who investigated the deaths refrained from editorial comment in making their reports. Fortunately I found reports that treated the aftermath of the event in more detail, and prefects who were less circumspect in presenting their accounts.

When seventeen-year-old Josephine Comte threw herself from a precipice with a scream loud enough to draw the attention of her companions, no one thought it odd that she had paused long enough before jumping to kiss the portrait of a penniless officer of whom she was enamored, or that she had taken the precaution of writing to her lover earlier that day, instructing him to come before two o'clock if he wanted to see her alive. Instead she was described in the prefect's report as the victim of her love, and mention was made of the refusal of Josephine's parents to approve a match between their daughter and a man without fortune, and of the officer's culpable failure to respond to the poor girl's note.[15]

Court-martialed for an illicit liaison he was conducting with a married woman in Calais, where his regiment was stationed,

Baron Philippou, colonel of the Legion of the Somme, shot himself rather than face the punishment his behavior merited. Before doing so, he wrote a note in which he pardoned his rival, whom he had earlier challenged to a duel, and described the act he was about to commit as motivated by his sense of honor: "Victim this day of the cruelest injustice, at least I have courage enough to exercise the only option that still remains, that of ending my days, my heart beating in joy to have finished my career in an honorable fashion. . . ." Philippou undertook to sacrifice himself rather than engage in a duel because he could not, in good conscience, "deprive a young woman of her hus- band and a child of his father," he wrote. His decision shows evidence of cunning as well, for in the sentimental realm in which he would ultimately be judged, the coolly calculated su- icide of honor counted more than the duel, which was of pas- sionate inspiration. And in fact, though Philippou's fellow officers had roundly condemned his immoral liaison, he received a military funeral. The prefect of the Pas-de-Calais further noted that he was buried with the bouquet that had been placed in his hands, presumably by his married lover.[16]

In both these examples it is clear that Romantic formulas were adopted, with great success, to lend nobility to the act of suicide, conferring upon Josephine Comte the mantle of a tragic heroine and granting the discredited Philippou a posthumous dignity he would not otherwise have attained. Observers of these events, townspeople and prefects, played a role in the dramas as well, their credulity enabling my subjects to be re- membered more or less as they chose to portray themselves. Not only did the audience share the suicides' artistic tastes; in some instances they demonstrated a creative impulse of their own. Describing a brutal murder followed by suicide that took place in a town under his jurisdiction, the prefect of the Drôme prefaced his report in the following way: "A double crime has come to afflict the town of Montélimar, which was its theatre. The fruit of immorality and of guilty passion, it carried with it the character of a base jealousy, revenged by a cruel attack. . . ." The tale of two lovers who swallowed poison together and were found sharing a bed in an inn was drawn in delicate detail by the prefect of the Nord, who ended his story of "ambition, love and contrariety" by describing how it was that the two "decided to play the tragic note that sent them to the tomb." And the literary ambitions of the prefect of the Oise were given an outlet in the recounting of the suicide of a young soldier:

> Reboul, Barthelemy, Dragoon of the Royal Guard, had conceived, in 1817, a strong passion for one *fille* Thuard, more appropriate in the role of concubine than in that of spouse; his parents would not permit him to marry this woman, and the duties of his service sent him away from her. Upon obtaining verbal permission from his unit for a leave, Reboul came back the fourth of this month to find the *fille* Thuard, who claimed that she no longer loved him. "Very well then!" Reboul said. "There remains nothing but to die!" Entering his inn that evening, he asked for [some cleaning fluid] on the pretext of needing to remove a stain from some soiled clothes. Having added to the coal provided for his use a sprinkle of this combustible substance which he deliberately took, he closed himself in his room, wrote with his blood a few lines in despair to his mistress, a few lines of reproach to his mother, and lay down on a mattress where he was asphyxiated by the accumulation of carbon gas.[17]

The thwarted passion that figured so prominently in the works of the Romantics was apparently perceived as the most justifiable grounds for self-destruction, judging from the predominance of the motif both in the suicides' own characterization of their plight and the ways in which their situations were described by outside observers. But dying for love did not always meet with society's approval. Fictional characters might escape the strictures of moral custom; no small part of the Romantic hero's appeal lay in his willingness to challenge traditional codes of decorum. But the self-styled heroes and heroines of everyday life were still judged by those codes, and in the majority of cases tradition won out over artistic license, particularly where the young were concerned.

In 1820 a twenty-two-year-old man in the Puy de Dôme and his married lover, a woman "already thirty-eight years old"—over the hill, in other words—asphyxiated themselves with coal fumes. While not condoning the woman's behavior ("nobody has come forward to accuse the husband of too much severity toward his wife"), the prefect reserved his sharpest criticism for the boy. "He was from a good family, but said to be given over to libertinage. It didn't take much to bring him to this extreme." The prefect of the Meuse expressed similar disapproval of the moral character of a young man who committed suicide in 1823, allegedly on account of an unrequited love affair. Etienne Duchesne hanged himself after being reprimanded by his father for drunkenness. "This young man was known to frequent bad company. He abandoned himself to wine," the prefect severely noted. Duchesne's own rather poetic version of his misery ("At fourteen I knew love, at twenty I became its slave, and at twenty-four it has driven me mad") was appended to the report without comment. And the prefect of the Rhône defended the uncle of a twenty-two-year-old man who shot himself rather than give up his mistress, of whom the uncle disapproved. "Monsieur Blatin, the uncle, who is very highly regarded in this city and who has been like a father to this nephew, is desolated by this event which he could not have prevented."[18]

The suicide of a son or daughter was seen not so much as a tragedy but as an affront: a deliberate assault on parental authority that not even the most heartrending effort at self-justification could disguise. A popular novel from the period, *The Last Day of a Suicide*, gives dramatic expression to this view. The story concerns the events leading up to a twenty-five-year-old man's decision to end his life and ends with his mother's reaction to her son's death. "He who has a mother and who kills himself possesses a stamp of character which may approach firmness, but which should not be confused with courage," the author admonishes. "This woman, whom God bestowed with so much love for her child, you wound to the heart in dying voluntarily before her, and if the wound is not immediately mortal, yet she will remain incurable, always bleeding, a butcher's knife lodged in her flesh."[19] The visceral force of that butcher's knife in poor mother's flesh seems overdone, but the violence behind it was not exaggerated. The archives provided many examples of young people who wielded death as a weapon against their parents.

Augustine Ragot drowned herself in 1829 while on a visit home. The twenty-year-old domestic was believed to have a boyfriend in her own town, but her parents sent her into service in another village in an attempt to separate the two. "You will never see me again," she warned them on the day she died. In 1824 an unemployed twenty-two-year-old man shot himself in his family home. His father had been pressing him to get a job, but he was too "weak-minded" and "disorganized" to find work, according to the prefect of the Ardennes. "Tomorrow will be my last day on earth," he threatened. It was the only promise he ever kept. By far the most vindictive example I came across was the letter a young man sent to his widowed mother in Lyères on the day he killed himself. The note begins respectfully enough: "You are the only person in the world I will miss in leaving for the glory of heaven," the son claims, but a few sentences later he plunges in the knife: "Alas, unfortunately for me, what drives me to end my career, alas, dear mother who never believed in me: what you think I have I don't have, except for two hundred and three francs—no lie—with which I will appear before God with no difficulty. . . ."[20]

I am struck by the contradiction, in each of these performances, between the willfulness of the gesture—the aggressive impulse behind that son's letter or the servant girl's threat— and the passive tone in which it was conveyed. As in the case of Goethe, the dishonesty, self-pity, and sheer malice that seem so obvious to me were camouflaged, to the apparent satisfaction of the actors and actresses involved, by the Romantic language they employed. They saw themselves as sufferers, victims who had no choice but to die. Like Sand's sensitive hero Sténio, they were too fine for this world, too pure. Pain purified them. A scorpion, encircled by flames, will pierce itself with its own stinger. "When a man dies in that way, is it truly suicide?" asked the poet Alfred de Vigny. "It's society that threw him into the blaze."[21]

Vigny posed the question in the Preface to *Chatterton*, his play about the impoverished seventeen-year-old English poet who committed suicide in 1770. The author of an intricate medieval saga that he tried to pass off as the work of a fifteenth-century monk, and a handful of poems and essays published under his own name, Thomas Chatterton is known today because his short life and poignant death captured the attention of nearly all the great English Romantics. Coleridge, Keats, Shelley, Byron, Wordsworth, and Rossetti composed poems in tribute to his memory. Here he is in "Resolution and Independence," an early poem of Wordsworth's:

> I thought of Chatterton, the marvelous Boy,
> The sleepless Soul that perished in his pride.

For Keats, who would also die young, Chatterton was "the Most English of Poets except Shakespeare," an unappreciated genius whose restless spirit infused the greatest works of Keats's own age:

> O Chatterton! How very sad thy fate!
> Dear child of sorrow—son of misery!
> How soon the film of death obscur'd that eye,
> Whence Genius mildly flash'd and high debate.

Coleridge, too, lamented the injustice of Chatterton's fate with a good many exclamation points:

> Sweet Flower of Hope! Free Nature's genial child!
> That dids't so fair disclose thy early bloom,
> Filling the wide air with a rich perfume!

For thee in vain all heavenly aspects smil'd;
From the hard world brief respite could they win.[22]

The tragedy of the marvelous boy's career inspired not only
poetry but also a famous painting by Henry Wallis, *The Death
of Chatterton*, which hangs in London's Tate Gallery, and a stream
of Victorian elegies, drawings, engravings, at least two monu-
ments, and various bits of memorabilia. A series of biographies
and creative reworkings of the story, beginning with *Love and
Madness*, a novel published by Herbert Croft in 1780, and culminating with Peter Ackroyd's 1987 best-seller *Chatterton*, attest
to the extraordinary and enduring mystique surrounding the
young poet's death. *Love and Madness*, the title of Croft's book,
gives an idea of what the fuss was all about. To anyone steeped
in Greek antiquity, as the English Romantics were, it evokes
Plato's discussion of divine madness, a state of grace shared by
artist and lover alike: "Because he stands apart from the common objects of human ambition and applies himself to the divine, he is reproached by most men for being out of his wits;
they do not realize that he is in fact possessed by a god."[23] The
madness of poets and lovers was no ordinary insanity, as Socrates' own example demonstrates. The voices he claimed to hear
throughout his life did not originate inside his head. They were
the gods' voices: intimations of a higher realm of absolutes
where truth resided and beauty reigned supreme. Only the purest souls were allowed a glimpse of this realm; lovers and artists
were visited by the truth, possessed by the muses, and mysti-
cally transported beyond the concerns of what Plato called the
sunlit world. But the insights they obtained in their moments
of divine inspiration were fleeting and almost impossible to con-

vey in words. Some spent their whole lives trying. Others, like poor Chatterton, unable to reconcile the perfection of his artistic vision with the grubby reality he inhabited, burned out in despair. Or so the story goes.[24]

For Croft, who somehow managed to weave Chatterton's story into his barely fictionalized account of the 1779 murder of the Earl of Sandwich's mistress by a deranged clergyman, the madness of the young poet was less exalted. Some of the details he included were in fact quite sordid, but his decision to publish Chatterton's letters in their entirety as part of his biographical sketch allowed later admirers to embellish the legend by drawing on the poet's own words. Indeed, it was Chatterton himself who introduced the "misunderstood genius" motif into the interpretation of his own life. In a fake *Last Will and Testament* he concocted some months before his actual suicide as part of a ploy to scare his employer into releasing him from his apprenticeship as a lawyer's clerk, he paraded his alleged insanity as a virtue:

> This is the last Will and Testament of me Thomas Chatterton of the City of Bristol being sound in Body or it is the Fault of my last Surgeon. The Soundness of my Mind the Coroner and Jury are to be judges of—desiring them to take notice that the most perfect Masters of Human Nature in Bristol, distinguish me by the Title of Mad Genius therefore if I do a mad action it is conformable to every Action of my Life which all savored of Insanity.

The *Last Will and Testament* reads like a parody of a legal document. Much of it was written in rhyming couplets, affectionate farewells to family members and friends, flirtatious lines to his many sweethearts mingling with spiteful if clever complaints—and Chatterton did not hesitate to name names—against all who failed to recognize or finance his talent. Although it comes across like the work of a seventeen-year-old with an inflated sense of his own importance, a carefully crafted piece of irony rather than the product of an addled brain, the ruse worked, and Chatterton was released from his obligations. His actual death by his own hand confirmed the insanity and ensured his immortality. A short story he published in a London magazine, *Town and Country*, unearthed by Robert Southey and Joseph Cottle in their 1803 edition of Chatterton's works, was taken as the sincere expression of his attitude toward self-destruction. "Suicide," he claimed, "is sometimes a noble insanity of the soul."[25]

The Chatterton style of self-destruction—that "noble insanity of the soul"—was the hallmark of the Romantic sensibility. Self-destruction was a marker of cultural refinement, the privilege of great lovers and gifted but fragile souls, of the young and talented especially, and this assumption persisted well beyond the Romantic era. Raphael Valentin, Balzac's earnest hero, was no more ridiculous than Flaubert's Madame Bovary or Eugène Sue's Gérard in *The Seven Deadly Sins*, both mid-century critiques of the Romantic type. When his mother hears that Gérard intends to commit suicide, her only response is to remark, "Yes, as in I can no longer remember which melodrama."[26] But not every character who yearned to die aristocratically was made to appear ridiculous. In *Axël*, the late-nineteenth-century symbolist play of Philippe August Villiers de l'Isle-Adam, suicide is depicted as the most sublime gesture a noble soul can make. The hero and heroine of Villiers's drama are the last descendants of two ancient, princely families, destined for centuries to come together and inherit their ancestral treasure. Axël and Sara meet and fall in love in the final act of the play, but rather than celebrate their union they drink poison together and die as the sun rises. Reality cannot approach the purity of their ideals. "It is the earth, don't you see, that has become the illusion . . . ," Axël reveals to his lover. "Live? Our servants will do that for us."

Axël's ennui was essentially Platonic, as the remainder of his speech makes clear: "Sated for an eternity, let us rise from the table and, in all fairness, leave the crumbs of our feast to be picked up by those hapless creatures who, by nature, cannot measure the value of realities by anything but sensation."[27] The pose of world-weariness so often adopted by artists and writers and by teenagers everywhere was a key feature of the Romantic sensibility. Would-be Chattertons admired the young man's refusal to settle for an ordinary career and longed for nothing more, it would seem, than to perish in their pride. In May 1827 a kitchen boy in the Seine et Marne left two suicide notes, one for his employer and one for a fellow servant, and disappeared. "I beg you to forgive me for leaving you in this position at the very moment when you are expecting company," he apologized to his master, "but it has become impossible for me to do otherwise." To his friend he went on at greater length, asking him to communicate his regrets to the count and countess "for no longer being able to serve them in leaving this world," giving detailed instructions on how his possessions were to be distributed, all while contriving to suggest that the job of servant was beneath him. The boy was presumed to have committed suicide, but when no body turned up, a search was launched and he was eventually found, arrested, and sent home to his parents.[28]

Naturally such "Chattertonesque" gestures, even those that really ended in death, were condemned. "I have already noted, with pain, along with Monsieur the Mayor of Sainte-Laurent, that attempts of this nature have been multiplying at an alarming rate for several years," the prefect of the Haute Vienne proclaimed in his 1828 investigation of the suicide of a farm laborer. This "horrible mania for suicide" among a class "that once held more sensibly to existence" should prompt "sad reflections," in his view. The tone of the prefect's denunciation leads me to think that the real crime, when a member of the lower class took his life, was not suicide but the inappropriate social aspirations that motivated it—a bias I found in several reports. A worker's son who had received a good education and was given free violin lessons because he showed talent killed himself, according to the prefect of the Cher, because he was invited only at the last minute to a luncheon that the well-born youngsters of the town were attending. "Very touchy, he observed with profound distress the obstacles that were placed in his way, on account of his humble origins, when he sought full admission to a higher rank of society." The prefect of the Sarthe, on the other hand, found it difficult to accept what he'd heard about the motivations for the suicide of a grocer's apprentice. "It is said that grief over not being well enough dressed for the city brought him to this act of despair."[29]

A good many nineteenth-century writers believed that suicide should remain the province of the elite. In his authoritative 1856 study, *Du Suicide et de la folie suicide*, Dr. Alexandre Brierre de Boismont attempted to combat the increasing incidence of self-destruction among the lower classes by deromanticizing the act. Having analyzed close to five thousand cases, Brierre confidently ascribed the vast majority to moral weakness or to insanity—to garden-variety madness, that is, as opposed to divine inspiration. In rare instances he allowed that a great and selfless impulse might lead heroic individuals to take their own lives, but there was a profound difference, he argued, between the melancholic who killed himself while under the delusion that he was being pursued by invisible enemies, or the man who sold his wife into prostitution and shot himself "when this infamous resource ran out," and the suicide of honor, such as he illustrated in the following example:

> A soldier, obliged by a revolutionary change in regime to leave his post because he would not fight to uphold a principle he detested, found no other distraction in his changed circumstances, and in the ensuing boredom, than gambling. The obsession devoured him. After several years of elation and despair, of resolutions and remorse, he managed to pause. Coldly he examined the situation: half of his fortune was lost, but there remained enough to raise his son and to assure an honest ease to his wife. "I profited from this flash of reason," he wrote, "to prevent your ruin." And he fell, struck by a bullet.

Brierre related the story of the unfortunate soldier in the Preface and returned to it frequently throughout his book, regarding the case as the benchmark against which less idealistic acts should be measured. "Certainly the principle is false," he commented in a later chapter, "since one can always reform, but what devotion and, one is tempted to say, what logic in [the soldier's] decision!" The suffering that the soldier experienced as a result of his addiction to gambling was of a higher order than the misery that accounted for most of the working-class suicides Brierre described. While acknowledging that hunger, need, and the inability to support oneself by honest means drove many poor people to take their lives, he nonetheless maintained that a large portion of these, "without a doubt, were conducted to this terrible resolution through laziness, a lack of foresight, libertinage, and drunkenness." Poverty, laziness, alcoholism, and unemployment evidently went hand in hand; all were the result of misconduct, of "bad morals," in Brierre's scheme. For every destitute parent who committed suicide in the hope that the act would draw charitable attention to his or her family's plight, for each proud soul who preferred death to the dishonor of begging, there were many, many more whose deaths were inspired by disgust for any form of gainful employment. Among these, Brierre mentioned a class of individuals among whom laziness appeared to be endemic: domestics. If there were some good Christians who became servants for the right reasons, most did so only out of a "horror for work." The maxim is still true, he concluded, that prosperity belongs to those who are motivated by a goal and work diligently to achieve it.

Given Brierre's insensitivity to the problems that might lead a poor individual to commit suicide, combined with his willingness to ascribe noble motives to those, like the soldier, who possessed enough of a fortune to gamble and lose, I am tempted to say that he reserved his pity for the self-destructive members of his own class. But there were limits to Brierre's indulgence for the suicides of the well-to-do, as his discussion of ennui makes plain. To those overly sensitive young men who had grown tired of living, he recommended that they get married and father a few children. Regular habits and the sweet compensations of family life would soon offset the inclination to wallow in their own misery. "And then, as if by magic, the demon of ennui will vanish." In Brierre's view, Werther's petulence, Chatterton's conceit, the languid dispositions of René and Raphaël were but artistic manifestations of the same selfish individualism that gave domestics ideas above their station.[30] And this, I believe, is why so many nineteenth-century writers—including the Romantics themselves—were critical of the literary conventions surrounding self-destruction.

What happened when the Romantic sensibility was diffused among the population at large? Gestures that seemed poetic on the page were deeply troubling in real life. Every Chatterton was someone's son and someone's employee, after all, and a death like Werther's left scars, as Goethe well knew. The more compelling the narrative, the more difficult it became to confront the aggressive impulse behind it, and this was true not only on the individual level. The democratization of suicide had dangerous social implications. In earlier times, noted a Paris physician in 1820, suicide had been the prerogative of the rich, who alone possessed the leisure to indulge in "morbid contemplation" and "egoistic despair." But now that the spirit of equality had infused even workers with ambition, "each aspires to the odious honor of being his own assassin." The real problem, according to Adelaide Celliez, Comtesse de Rossi, was class ambition. Artisans, shopkeepers, bourgeois citizens—all were corrupted by greed, viewing life in terms of profit and loss instead of appreciating what they had. The "peaceful happiness" of middle-class life should be preservative enough against suicide, she maintained, but too many people preferred death to a life in which "bourgeois tastes" remained unfulfilled.[31]

Emile Durkheim shared this view of suicide. The discontent that prompted the Romantic hero to end his life was endemic to modern society: a consequence of a culture in which a self-centered individualism prevailed. His *Le Suicide* appeared in 1897, long after the Romantic vogue had subsided, yet the sociologist still claimed that the literary creations of Lamartine, Goethe, and Chateaubriand offered the best illustrations of his two famous typologies, the egoistic and anomic modes of suicide. Having lost the sense of belonging to his society, Raphaël represented the egoistic type, *par excellence*. The morbid introspection in which the young man indulged, his quest for self-knowledge through the endless contemplation of his own pain, soon brought him to renounce the life in which he was doomed to remain incomplete.

Egoists like Raphaël detached themselves gently from existence. Suicide, for them, was merely the full realization of the emptiness they projected onto the world; sooner or later oblivion would catch up with them. In contrast to the passive acceptance of death that characterized Lamartine's hero, Durkheim maintained, the anomic individual was driven to destroy himself out of rage and frustration. Here it was not a case of simply allowing oneself to die; where an individual set his expectations too high, wanting more than he could realistically hope to obtain, he was destined to be disappointed. "A man abruptly cast down below his accustomed status cannot avoid exasperation at feeling a situation escape him of which he thought himself master," he wrote, "and his exasperation naturally revolts against the cause, whether real or imaginary, to which he attributes his ruin."[32]

Werther's suicide was exemplary in this respect. There was a restlessness in Goethe's hero, a sense that nothing would satisfy his overwhelming needs. In the opinion of W. H. Auden, Werther was nothing less than "a spoiled brat, incapable of love because he cares for nobody and nothing but himself and having his way at whatever cost to others." Auden was not moved in the least by Werther's plight. "What a horrid little monster!" he exclaimed.[33] The monstrousness that Auden identified— Durkheim described it more neutrally, as "the infinity of desires"—was the key ingredient of anomie. Unrestrained wants, an insatiable appetite for new experiences and sensations, combined with a nervous temperament, were all features of the Romantic spirit, and Durkheim regarded them as the dominant characteristics of his own age as well. "Is it my fault if I everywhere find limits, if everything once experienced has no value for me?" This complaint of René's epitomized the anomic personality, according to Durkheim. I find it remarkable that the eminent sociologist, a self-proclaimed rationalist for whom "too literary" was the highest term of abuse,[34] should have resorted to such sentimental examples to support his theory. But perhaps it is not so surprising. The great appeal of Romantic narratives lay in their completeness, in the clean resolution that a well-crafted story provides. *Werther* ends unhappily with the hero's suicide, but for those readers who were affected by Werther's plight, closure was achieved through Goethe's rendering of his character's suffering. And the knowledge that Goethe had experienced the very same sadness is what gave the work authority.

Durkheim accepted the Romantics' authority on the subject of suicidal despair and was drawn, somewhat against his will, I suspect, into the Romantic vision of the artist as Prometheus, "suffering," as Joyce Carol Oates once put it, "more eloquently than ordinary men and suffering, in fact, for the benefit of ordinary men."[35] Even today the allure of the Promethean artist is hard to resist. In *Darkness Visible,* William Styron's account of the depression that nearly brought him to kill himself, the writer talks about the impulse that allows the suffering artist to turn his torment into a thing of beauty and ultimately "to vanquish death through work honored by posterity." The assumption that artists feel more deeply than ordinary mortals and that greatness resides in their ability to transform pain into poetry is central to his book. "In many of Albrecht Dürer's engravings there are harrowing depictions of his own melancholia," Styron writes; "the manic wheeling stars of Van Gogh are the precursors of the artist's plunge into dementia and the extinction of self. It is suffering that often tinges the music of Beethoven, of Schumann and Mahler, and permeates the darker cantatas of Bach."

Styron credits himself with the same ability. "In rereading, for the first time in years, sequences from my novels    passages where my heroines have lurched down pathways toward doom— I was stunned to perceive how accurately I had created the landscape of depression in the minds of these young women," he tells us. And then, in an eerie sentence, he goes on to describe his illness as a guest who arrives unbidden: "Thus depression, when it finally came to me, was in fact no stranger, not even a visitor totally unannounced; it had been tapping at my door for decades." The experiencing of madness as a visitation—although there is nothing of the divine in Styron's account of his paralyzing mental pain—is very much in the Romantic tradition, and the association is only strengthened by Styron's acknowledgment of the "theatrical quality" of his suicide attempt. "I couldn't shake off a sense of melodrama," he admits, "a melodrama in which I, the victim-to-be of self-murder, was both the solitary actor and lone member of the audience."

I do not mean to diminish the terror of Styron's depression by emphasizing the clichéd elements of his narrative. There is certainly no enjoyment in the way he relates his ordeal. The brief glimpse he provides into the utterly hopeless state of mind he endured for months on end, the hours spent in bed, staring blankly at the ceiling, the nameless fears that obsessed him when he went outdoors, his clinging to his wife in the supermarket, was disturbing enough to read about. I cannot imagine how it felt. But every so often an aesthetic awareness creeps into the story, as if to remind readers that he was no ordinary sufferer.

Styron could not write a suicide note, he says. The artist in him rebelled at the banality of the gesture, and the only words he was capable of composing sounded pompous and inelegant to his ear. In Paris, where he first contemplated suicide, he found himself thinking about the depressed French artists he knew: Albert Camus, Romain Gary, and Gary's estranged wife, the American actress Jean Seberg. This leads into a digression on famous suicides, culminating in a selective "roll call" of fallen artists: Hart Crane, Vincent Van Gogh, Virginia Woolf, Arshile Gorky, Cesare Pavese. . . . Although Styron refrains from adding his name to the list, when moving from his personal experience to a more general survey of depression he cannot resist pointing out "that artistic types (especially poets) are particularly vulnerable to the disorder—which, in its graver, clinical manifestation takes upward of twenty percent of its victims by way of suicide." *Darkness Visible* ends with a consoling line of Dante's. *And so we came forth, and once again beheld the stars.* Styron wants to reassure his readers that depression is curable. The consolation for him, I believe, was not merely that he emerged from the darkness of his depression but that he was able to write about it, to find the words, at last, to convey his story.[36]

Kay Redfield Jamison does much the same thing in her memoir of manic-depression, *An Unquiet Mind*. "The Chinese believe that before you can conquer a beast you must first make it beautiful," she states. "In some strange way I have tried to do that with manic-depressive illness." Jamison admits her reluctance to view the darkness at either extreme the bleak depression and the violent mania she experienced—as part of herself. Yet she acknowledges the exhilarating creativity of her manic moods: "I tend to compare my current self with the best I have been, which is when I have been mildly manic." Both *An Unquiet Mind* and her study of suicide, *Night Falls Fast*, are studded with quotations from depressed artists; she too offers a list—longer than Styron's, and in alphabetical order—of eminent artists, writers, "especially poets," and scientists who committed suicide. And in her discussion of the hereditary influences on madness in general and suicide in particular, Jamison speculates on the evolutionary advantage that extreme states confer. "The boldness and violence of the manic temperament may come at a cost," she admits, "but there is strong evidence that manic-depression and its milder forms can provide advantages to the individual, his or her kin, and society at large." Fearlessness, risk-taking, and aggression—the very qualities that drive people to destruction—are traits that benefit the species.

"Clearly, mood disorders are not required for great accomplishments, and most people who suffer from mood disorders are not particularly accomplished," she concedes. "But the evidence is compelling that the creative are *disproportionately* affected by these conditions."[37]

Creativity has its price, but madness has its compensations. For those possessed by *The Savage God*, as Alfred Alvarez titled his memoir of suicide, "the better the artist, the more vulnerable he seems to be." Alvarez provides several lists of vulnerable artists in his book: famous suicides in the ancient world, artists who died young, though not necessarily by their own hand, artists who survived a midlife crisis to produce their finest work, artists who chose not to survive under totalitarian regimes, and self-destructive twentieth-century novelists, painters, and poets—especially poets—who courted death in various ways, some more actively than others. Alvarez gives us Sylvia Plath, who was able to write about the violence of her innermost self, pouring her life's blood onto the page, all in the cause of art. "The authority of her poetry," he tells us, "was in part due to her brave persistence in following the thread of her inspiration right down to the Minotaur's lair." In place of the messy complex of motivations that led Plath to gas herself in her kitchen with her two children sleeping upstairs, we are given a seductive combination of sensitivity and recklessness, suffering and redemption. Alvarez in fact, discourages us from looking too closely at Plath's reasons for killing herself. "It was an act she felt she had a right to as a grown woman and a free agent," he insists. ". . . Because of this there was never any question of motives: you do it because you do it, just as an artist always knows what he knows."[38]

The artist knows there is always an audience. From the closely observed world of the nineteenth-century French village to the popular genre of memoir literature today, the stories that work are the ones that meet their audience's expectations. But what audiences expect is not necessarily the truth; wholeness in a story is often achieved by leaving things out: ugly things, messy things, mean and self-serving justifications, bleak realities the suicide cannot or will not face. The modern gloss on the Romantic script has not progressed much beyond Goethe and Chatterton. That noble insanity of the soul is still heroic, still persuasive, and, in its modern reincarnation, supremely satisfying to actor and audience alike.

# Tragic Artists

I SAY it began with a mystery, my decision to study suicide in graduate school and later, when I was teaching history in Ohio, to volunteer on a suicide hotline. My grandfather killed himself in 1938. The son of an Austrian rabbi, he had come to America as a young man and started a business selling fruit. His business failed during the depression, and he lost all his savings when the banks collapsed. By the autumn of 1938 he could no longer cover the premium on his life insurance policy and was afraid it would lapse, so he went down to the basement, put his head in the oven, and turned on the gas. He left a wife and eight children. My father, the youngest of those children, was fifteen years old.

When I was growing up, my father would follow the Jewish custom of lighting a memorial candle on the anniversary of his father's death to keep the memory alive. We never talked about my grandfather at any other time; I have no impression of what he was like. Did he smoke? Did he tell jokes? Was he ever happy? What kind of parent was he? I wonder most about this last question, now that I am a parent myself. But all I have is the fact of my grandfather's suicide: the mystery that haunted my childhood.

On the hotline we were trained to listen for specific things, for example whether the caller had a precise plan for ending his life and whether he possessed the means to do it. Within the first five minutes we had to make an assessment of the caller's lethality. Was he likely to attempt suicide within the next hour? Within twenty-four hours? Or was he mainly in need of a sympathetic ear? Our answer to these questions determined the strategy we would pursue for the remainder of the call. Highly lethal callers had to be distanced from the means immediately, then talked down and encouraged to get help. With the others we had more time. Most people who call a service advertising itself as a suicide prevention hotline don't really want to stop living. They just want to stop the pain. Our job was to help them find ways to do that without hurting themselves.

Every call was a story with a mystery at its heart: the question of why the person at the other end of the line wanted to die. Answering this question was the next thing we were supposed to do. Behind the grief and anger, which the callers had to express in order to breathe, was the still point at the center I would listen for, the thing that told me why they hated themselves. Once I found it, we could work together toward a resolution, a way of getting them through the night at first, then maybe through the following days. Sometimes I never found it, the source of the caller's self-hatred. Sometimes all I could hear was the pain and rage. And sometimes this rage seemed directed against me for not being able to help. These calls troubled me as I drove home on Saturday nights at the end of my shift. The lack of resolution, both for the caller and for myself, was almost unbearable, and it took time to distance myself from the anxieties it provoked.

What I felt on those midnight drives and in the face of the silence surrounding my grandfather's death is what we all feel when we are confronted by suicide. The helplessness, the guilt, and the constant wondering—these are common reactions to the trauma of suicide. Self-destruction changes forever our relationship to the person who died, fixing it at a point beyond understanding and making closure impossible. And this is no less true of the tragic artists and intellectuals who kill themselves than of the suicides who touch our personal lives.

We are drawn to tormented artists. We seek them out, watching, fascinated, as they play the line where self-destructiveness verges into suicide. The ragged quality of Billie Holiday's voice in her final years. Sylvia Plath's rendering of her suicide attempts in "Lady Lazarus." Hemingway's drinking. Baudelaire's drugs. Van Gogh's ear. Why should the evidence of an artist's pain affect us so profoundly while the greater abundance of human misery leaves us cold? Posed starkly, this question sounds like an indictment, a severe appraisal of our indifference to the suffering of our fellow creatures. Yet it is precisely such questions that mattered most to the figures I most admire. The willingness of artists and intellectuals to confront injustice, their ability to understand cruelty, to shed light on the darkest realms of human experience, and from these depths to derive meaning: all stem from a harsh awareness of their own failings. To recognize the destructive source of creativity is to acknowledge not only why we expect great artists to suffer but why they also seem to expect it of themselves.

All her life Diane Arbus battled the security of her privileged upbringing. The private-school education, Palm Beach vacations, Fifth Avenue shopping sprees. She wanted to feel something, to break through the protective shell she had been encased in since childhood and experience life in all its awfulness and gritty splendor. "I never suffered from adversity," she told Studs Terkel. "I was confirmed in a sense of unreality." Arbus's obsession with the kind of people she had been told not to stare at, the people most of us instinctively avoid—freaks, misfits, deviants, and the mentally retarded—grew out of a belief that reality entails pain and horror. To be an artist meant putting yourself in the way of danger, living always in a keyed-up state, ever alert to the fleeting beauty that resides in the strange and ugly, the eeriness of the mundane. "She liked being afraid because there was in it the possibility of something terrific," her daughter explained.[1]

Arbus's suicide has been seen as the price she paid for venturing into the realm of the forbidden. As Susan Sontag ironically notes in *On Photography*, ". . . it proved the photographs to have been dangerous to her."[2] Arbus's images are certainly disturbing: the dwarves, giants, drag queens, nudists, tattooed men, and retarded adults who became her trademark. When her work was first exhibited at the Museum of Modern Art in New York, curators had to clean the spit off the pictures each day, so repelled were patrons by the subject matter and Arbus's refusal to soften her gaze, to permit viewers to look away. But what lingers in my mind now that the initial shock has worn off are not only Arbus's freaks. Once I saw her photographs of crying babies, tacky suburban couples, parade watchers, shoppers, the rich and famous caught off-guard, I could never look at normal people in quite the same way. Nothing was sacred; everything was grotesque to her eye. "Beauty is itself an aberration," she claimed.[3]

Arbus's opus may be viewed as cynical commentary on the hypocrisy of American society in the fifties and early sixties. Here the photographer becomes the brave crusader against bourgeois complacency, the defender of the marginalized and misunderstood, the speaker of truths no one is willing to hear. At times Arbus encouraged this interpretation of her work, embracing the role of iconoclast and bragging about her bad-girl antics. More often, however, she seemed perplexed by all the attention. Arbus was plagued by self-doubt. Her most productive period was also a time of chronic depression, bouts of despair alternating with spells of intense productivity. Eventually the despair overwhelmed her, and she lost the will to create. "My work doesn't do it for me anymore," she told a friend on the eve of her suicide. Was it merely a desire to shock people that led her to photograph the subjects she did? A compulsion to look at the most horrible things without flinching, as Sontag suggests? Or was it not also a wish to punish herself for having been immune, for so long, to the suffering of others?[4]

Self-hatred was at the core of Arbus's vision. Her effort to enter the world of freaks and deviants, to conquer her squeamishness in order to earn their trust and convey their image to others, smacks of bourgeois guilt. In this she reminds me of other radicals from well-to-do backgrounds, notably the French philosopher, left-wing activist, and mystic Simone Weil. Born in 1909 into a wealthy Parisian Jewish family, Weil sought out contact with "the humiliated"—her term for the working class—going so far as to spend a year as a factory worker in the hope of experiencing affliction firsthand. Weil too made forays into the underworld. She once tried to accompany her male colleagues into a brothel to learn the prostitutes' milieu. In Spain she visited a cabaret and was enthralled by the transvestite performers. On the same trip she attended a bullfight, pronouncing the bloody spectacle beautiful. And she imagined for herself a heroic death in the mode of Seneca, who killed himself at the emperor Nero's command, resolute in the face of his friends' grief.

Weil's posthumous fame derives largely from the writings she produced during the final years of her life when she, a Jew by birth and an atheist by inclination, embraced Christianity after experiencing a mystical union with God. Suddenly her identification with the downtrodden, the year of factory work, made sense: "There I received forever the mark of slavery," she explained. She now saw that Christianity was the religion of slaves, "that slaves cannot help belonging to it, and I among others." This realization led her to redirect her energies. Though still committed to the goal of social reform, nothing less than the spiritual transformation of humanity would be required to bring it about.[5]

Weil was never a joiner. At the height of her involvement with left-wing politics she refused to enter either the Communist or Socialist party. She would later resist the efforts of her spiritual advisers to bring her into the church. What attracted her to a cause was not the opportunity to belong to a community of like-minded souls. Simone Weil was searching for truth. Her quest led her from one movement to the next, but she always came away empty handed. Her spirit was too restless, her intellect too penetrating to allow her to be satisfied with the orthodoxies preached to the converted, whether these took the form of Marxist doctrine or Catholic dogma. She was at her most brilliant in the role of disinterested critic, as in her famous essay "The Iliad, or the Poem of Force." In this piece, written in the months following the fall of France, she sets out to understand how human beings can commit acts of atrocity against one another. Her insight—that those who employ violence are no less brutalized by the experience than their victims—is both compassionate and profoundly pessimistic: compassionate in the empathy it shows toward the oppressor; pessimistic in its ultimate insistence that the capacity for cruelty exists in all of us.

Christianity satisfied Weil's deepest longing, confirming her feelings of worthlessness while providing her with the incentive to sacrifice herself for a noble cause. From the start, martyrdom was clearly what she had in mind. "At this moment," she wrote to the priest who wanted to baptize her, "I should be more ready to die for the Church, if one day before long it should need anyone to die for it, than I should be to enter it." Just before the German offensive, she had offered her services to the state as a battlefield nurse, fully expecting to be killed in the line of duty. Her offer was turned down, but eventually she succeeded in getting herself sent to London to work for the Free French. Once there, she begged to be parachuted back into France, seeking, as she put it, "some activity in the cannon-fodder line." When this opportunity too was denied, she made up her mind to live in England as if she were under German occupation, eating only as much as she believed her countrymen were eating, refusing to sleep, to heat her room in winter, or to accept anything that would make her appear privileged. Hospitalized with tuberculosis, she continued to starve herself and died in a few months of cardiac arrest.[6]

Weil's suicide has posed a problem for her admirers. She was not a tormented artist, after all, but an engaged intellectual whom both Catholics and the left have wanted to claim as their own. Arbus's friend, the photographer Richard Avedon, was heard to say at her funeral, "I wish I were an artist like Diane."[7] In contrast, Weil's friends went to great pains to prove that her death was not intentional, that the self-denial she practiced throughout her short life was not fanatic, that she was mentally stable to the end. Although harsher assessments have appeared, she continues to be regarded by many as a martyr to the cause of justice, as if she had indeed died, like Seneca, at another's command. Not merely her ideas but her character is exhibited as reason for taking her seriously, the need for saints overriding all efforts to paint a balanced portrait of this troubled thinker.

The reasons Weil and Arbus wanted to die are still a mystery. Other artists and intellectuals made peace with their bourgeois backgrounds. Why couldn't they? I follow them into the dark places they explored, trying to understand the masochism that fueled their work and ultimately destroyed them, but all I find is anger. Arbus gloried in her ability to remain detached from the people she slept with. Sex, for her, was an essential way of gaining the authentic experience she craved. Or so she claimed. Am I alone in seeing this behavior as hostile? In the same way, I keep returning to the most disturbing manifestation of Weil's self-hatred: her pronounced antagonism toward Judaism, the faith of her ancestors. The closer she drew to Christianity, the more she insisted on the need to purge the religion of its "Jewish impurities." In a report she composed in London not long before she died, she calmly recommended that French Jews be encouraged to intermarry with Christians so they would disappear as a distinct minority in a few generations—this at a time when Hitler was pursuing the same objective.[8]

To dwell on these matters is unpleasant, but as with the unresolved calls that stayed with me on the drive home from the hotline, I cannot seem to leave them alone. I sense a tension in the dynamic between altruism and guilt, a vital paradox that has never been fully explored. Only by turning against themselves, by aggressively pursuing experiences that caused them pain, did Weil and Arbus feel connected with other people. I cannot call this compassion, the zealous urge to suffer in solidarity with the oppressed. And yet I am reluctant to believe that Weil and Arbus destroyed themselves out of sheer frustration, unwilling to live with their powerlessness in the face of injustice. Believing this would deprive their deaths of meaning and thus diminish the value of both women's lives.

I am not unique in my hesitation. The tendency to read significance into an artist's suicide is irresistible. Look at the legend surrounding the poet Sylvia Plath. This artist who wrote so well and so frequently about dying and then proceeded to kill herself, as if she needed to get it right on paper before going through with the act, grows more popular all the time. Since 1990 nine biographies have appeared, supplementing the hundreds of scholarly articles, books, doctoral dissertations, and the many collections of her work already in print. Much as Weil satisfied the postwar yearning for spiritual commitment and Arbus embodied the alienation of the sixties, so Plath has been

celebrated as an early casualty in the war for women's liberation. Her poetry speaks to the dilemma of talented women
everywhere, a dilemma she proved incapable of resolving.
"Caught in a culture that devalued and disempowered her as a
woman and bound to a mother who was never able to achieve
the sense of separation and autonomy needed to help herself,
let alone her daughter," writes Paula Bennett in *My Life a Loaded
Gun*, "Sylvia Plath burnt herself out in rage."[9]

Plath's rage is impossible to ignore. It bubbles up in her
early work, foreshadowing the violence of the *Ariel* poems, her
best-known collection, written in the white heat of her abandonment by Ted Hughes. At times the violence is stark, its
beauty deriving from the complete absence of emotion, as in
the last image from "Burning the Letters":

> The dogs are tearing a fox. This is what it is like—
> A red burst and a cry
> That splits from its ripped bag and does not stop
> With the dead eye
> And the stuffed expression, but goes on
> Dyeing the air,
> Telling the particles of the clouds, the leaves, the water
> What immortality is. That it is immortal.

But there is a self-indulgent aspect to Plath's anger, a tendency
to luxuriate in her own misery. Repeatedly she evokes the Holocaust, filling her poems with by-products of the crematoria—
bones and ashes, soap, bits of gold extracted from the smol-
dering remains. "I think I may well be a Jew," she exclaims in
"Daddy," as if her unhappiness were on a par with the agony of
Hitler's victims. "I may be a bit of a Jew."

I admire Plath's audacity. The sheer power of her poetry, the force of her images, make the question of whether or not she, a non-Jew, had the right to speak of the Holocaust almost irrelevant. My reservations about Plath's use of the event have more to do with its effect upon her reputation than with the appropriateness or inappropriateness of the metaphor she chose to convey her pain. I see the borrowing as dishonest, not only because it trivializes the suffering of Hitler's victims but because it elevates Plath's suffering to such a peak that it becomes impossible to view her as anything but a victim. Which was, I think, precisely how she wanted it.

In "Edge," her final poem, written six days before she gassed herself in the kitchen of her London apartment, Plath sketches her closing scene:

The woman is perfected.
Her dead

Body wearing the smile of accomplishment,
The illusion of a Greek necessity

Flows in the scrolls of her toga,
Her bare

Feet seem to be saying:
We have come so far, it is over.

Each dead child coiled, a white serpent,
One at each little

Pitcher of milk, now empty.
She has folded

Them back into her body as petals
Of a rose close when the garden

Stiffens and odors bleed
From the sweet, deep throats of the night flower.

The moon has nothing to be sad about,
Staring from her hood of bone.

She is used to this sort of thing.
Her blacks crackle and drag.

Like Medea, Plath allows herself the satisfaction of exacting a complete revenge for her husband's betrayal. But when it came down to it, she did not take the children with her. Instead she took care to prevent the gas from seeping into their bedroom and even left food nearby for them to find when they woke up. This act of maternal tenderness is a crucial detail in the Plath legend. Never mind that Plath killed herself in the house where her small son and daughter were sleeping, that they might just as easily have found her dead body as the bread and milk she so thoughtfully placed in their bedroom. We should forgive the fury that drove her to turn on the gas because, at the very end, she showed concern for her children.

Perhaps Plath did not seriously intend to die in this, her third suicide attempt. More than one biographer has speculated that the poet's death was inadvertent: a cry for help that was not answered in time.[10] But given the pleasure she took in contriving her own destruction, it seems likely she would have tried again. "And like the cat I have nine times to die," she boasts in "Lady Lazarus," declaring, famously, a few stanzas later:

Dying
Is an art, like everything else.
I do it exceptionally well.

What is strange about the legend surrounding Plath's suicide is that it excludes the possibility that killing herself was an act of aggression. I am struck by the malice of "Daddy," the cold cruelty of "Edge." Few poets manage to sustain such intense wrath; few dare to expose the ugliness in themselves so completely. But I resist allowing this same ugliness—and Plath's evident relishing of it—a role in her death.

My fascination with Plath's suicide brings me into that cold kitchen in London. I watch, horrified, as she tapes the windows shut against the draft. Respectfully I follow behind as she carries milk and bread into her children's room, pausing over the sleeping forms in their little beds, but at the last minute I look away. I resist taking the next step with Plath because this step brings me too close to the source of my own self-destructive impulses. Rarely do any of us exult in thoughts of death as she liked to do. Like Arbus, we might test the boundaries from time to time. We might even share Weil's fantasy of dying, when we die, for a worthwhile cause. But whether we recognize it or not, the self-hating part inside all of us is never silent. What draws us to tragic artists, like rubberneckers to the scene of a crash, is the realization that we could have been in the wreck.

I say this, and all the while I am conscious of what I am leaving out. In different ways, Plath, Weil, and Arbus each tried to come to terms with evil, to understand it not as something alien but as an integral part of who she was. Drawn into the realm of their preoccupations, we are forced to confront the darkness within ourselves. We cling to the resolution that is usually offered in their works and are deeply troubled when they refuse to accept the same way out. Fear impels us to unravel the mystery of an artist's suicide: the fear of succumbing to our own violent impulses. And fear is what ultimately stops us short. Unless we can distance ourselves from the bitterness such deaths arouse, we too are condemned to the destructiveness of rage and despair.

The current reappraisal of Bruno Bettelheim's reputation is a case in point. But this time the stakes are higher, for the life and work of the Viennese child therapist were intricately tied to the Holocaust. Bettelheim first attracted notice for his innovative approach to the problem of autism, a technique he publicized in a succession of books that brought international attention to his Chicago school. His goal was to build a nurturing institution, a neutral, accepting environment where disturbed children would feel safe to resolve the inner conflicts that had caused them to retreat from the world. The notion that children have a dark side that they must be allowed to express before they can attain maturity is a commonplace of psychoanalysis, and Bettelheim happily acknowledged his debt to Freud. But he also proved capable of going beyond Freud on many occasions, taking liberties with the master's teachings in order to create works of a more poetic nature. *The Uses of Enchantment*, his most popular book, sets out to restore fairy tales to their rightful place on a child's bookshelf. Far from scaring children with their gruesome themes of cruelty and revenge, Bettelheim argues, these fantasies provide reassurance on the most basic level, enabling young readers to confront their fears so they can develop into productive adults.

By the time he died, Bettelheim had established himself as an expert on the emotional life of children. His opinions on family issues appeared regularly in magazines such as the *Atlantic Monthly, Parents, Harper's,* and the *New Yorker,* and for several years he wrote a monthly advice column for the *Ladies' Home Journal.* Not long after his suicide in 1990, however, he was accused of everything from falsifying his professional credentials and plagiarizing his best-known work to running his school like a dictator and mistreating the children under his care. A recent biography by Richard Pollak leaves little standing. *The Creation of Dr. B* painstakingly exposes the lies upon which Bettelheim based his career, honing in on the galvanizing experience of his life and the unique source of Bettelheim's authority: his status as a Holocaust survivor.[11]

For ten months between 1938 and 1939, Bettelheim was a concentration camp inmate. The brutality he experienced in Dachau and Buchenwald gave his life purpose, he would later write. It was here he learned what it meant to survive. Upon his release he vowed to put the insights he had gained studying his own reactions to the dehumanizing regime of the camps to good use, first by informing the world of the existence of such places and then by striving to negate their destructive effects by imbuing damaged children with the will to survive. Again and again Bettelheim returned to the subject of the camps to make the point that only by meeting force with force can one avoid becoming a victim. "All people, Jews or gentiles, who dare not defend themselves when they know they are in the right," he asserted in his notorious essay on ghetto thinking, ". . . are already dead by their own decision." He went on to castigate the six million Jews who perished in the gas chambers for the passivity that kept them from fleeing the *shtetls* of Eastern Europe or, in the last resort, from fighting back instead of marching obediently to their deaths.[12]

Of all the theories Bettelheim published, this was the most controversial, that strictly by their own behavior Jews had brought destruction upon themselves. During his lifetime Bettelheim was confronted by Holocaust survivors, inmates of Auschwitz, Sobibór, Treblinka, who had endured far worse conditions than he, including being subjected to the perpetual threat of extermination. They accused him of arrogance for daring to compare his experiences to theirs. Pollak spares no effort to prove this accusation just. Not only did Bettelheim manage to procure his release from Buchenwald in four months, but he apparently found ways of getting assigned to easy tasks during the six months he spent in Dachau. Not until September 1939, when he was safe in America, did Hitler fully implement his policy of annihilation. It does seem presumptuous for Bettelheim to have set himself up as an expert on the basis of his limited experience in camps not designed expressly for extermination. To then proceed to pass judgment on the dead, seeming to join forces with the anti-Semite, is absolutely unforgivable, and no amount of backpedaling in his subsequent essays can ever change that.

Still, I grapple with Bettelheim's views on survival and cannot stop, as Pollak does, with self-righteous condemnation. How could he say that Jews were to blame for the Holocaust, this man who weighed just eighty-six pounds when he left Buchenwald? What does this reveal about his own inability to face the truth? And why were so many conscientious souls, Jews included, persuaded by Bettelheim's arguments? The answer lies in an essay, "Children of the Holocaust," which appeared in the collection he compiled during the final year of his life. Describing the coping strategies employed by children who survived Nazi persecution, Bettelheim breaks off in an uncharacteristic moment of self-reflection: "I found myself during the year I spent at Dachau and Buchenwald in a somewhat similar situation [to that of the child whose memoir he was reviewing]. One was very sad when a comrade was murdered, but one did not shed tears, because one was oneself only a hairbreadth from death."

The awkwardness of Bettelheim's shift from the "I" of the first sentence to the impersonal "one" which takes over for the remainder of the paragraph is very telling. Indeed, it confirms the point of the essay, for Bettelheim's aim is to understand why Hitler's youngest victims came to repress their memories of trauma instead of mourning their losses. Borrowing a metaphor from one of the child survivors whose history he had been recounting, he explains how Holocaust victims buried their pain in an iron box within themselves, never daring to examine the contents for fear of what they would find. The iron box makes life possible and impossible at the same time. As long as the victims could deny what they felt during those horrible years, they would have the strength to survive. But always there is the awareness that something is terribly wrong. "Things thus repressed so deeply nevertheless seem to have an independent existence that corrodes one's life, destroys the right to enjoy things, even the feeling that one has a right to live," Bettelheim comments.[13]

That Bettelheim was scarred by his treatment at Dachau and Buchenwald is undeniable. Ten months is certainly long enough to grow habituated to a regime of senseless cruelty and to develop coping strategies such as the one described in "Children of the Holocaust." The fact that he managed to survive inside the camps, and later managed to get out, did not diminish the torments he experienced. On the contrary, this knowledge added guilt to the weight of painful memories he brought with him to America in 1939. Pollak's attempt to calibrate the survivor's suffering—so many undeserved beatings, so many dead companions, so many last-minute reprieves from the gas chambers equals a valid experience—is unfair. Bettelheim survived *because* he refused to let himself think about what was happening to him, both at the time and later. He survived, but he despised himself for surviving.

Remarkably, he was able to wrest meaning from his ordeal. In his books as in the therapeutic milieu he created in his school, he demonstrated that something worthwhile could be salvaged from the ashes, that optimism and compassion could triumph over despair and indifference at the worst of times. John Updike put his finger on the essence of Bettelheim's appeal in his review of *The Uses of Enchantment*. "While in the spell of this most benignly paternal scholar of our hearts," he wrote in the *New Yorker*, "we forget that his own enchanting presumption of life as a potentially successful adventure may be itself something of a fairy tale."[14]

Bettelheim himself never quite believed in the fairy tale. The dilemma, as he wearily acknowledged at the end of his life, was living with oneself afterward. After Dachau, after seeing the depths to which we and our fellow creatures will plunge in order to survive, how can we trust anything, ourselves, let alone another human being? There are times when outer survival can be accomplished only at the cost of inner survival, he tells us, times when the thirst for life entails the dissolution of everything that gives life value. I believe Bettelheim's suicide had the effect of affirming this bleak view of reality and negating his earlier optimism. We feel betrayed because he is no longer reassuring in that benignly paternal way; by destroying himself he destroyed all the comforting illusions he had constructed over the course of his therapeutic career, and for this we are not ready to forgive him.

Dismissing Bettelheim allows us to put distance between ourselves and the discomforting reflections his end inspires in us. What is more, it is easy to do since pity was the last thing he wanted. Bettelheim forgave nothing and could not bring himself to ask others to forgive him. By all accounts he was an angry man. And yet he succeeded in turning his anger to good purpose. He made a virtue of it, in fact. The heartlessness he displayed toward Holocaust victims, including even Anne Frank and her family, was compounded of his experiences as a camp inmate, but as one who refused to be identified as a victim or to allow what he suffered during those ten months to destroy what remained of his life. Never did Bettelheim grieve for what he lost in Dachau and Buchenwald. Admiration he sought and received, but not sympathy. Obviously he felt he did not deserve it.

In contrast to Plath and Weil, who strove to attain the status of victims, those writers who survived the Holocaust regarded their involuntary victimization with great ambivalence. On the one hand it made them angry, the memory of their ordeal, and to this anger they felt entitled. What could be more righteous than the anger of Hitler's victims? They felt anguish, too, for all those other victims, the ones who had suffered and died alongside them. But at the same time they were ashamed. Some memories are corrosive, even when they are repressed; Bettelheim recognized this truth but could do nothing to refute it. Even as he indulged his anger and attempted to deny his guilt by displacing the blame onto his fellow victims, he felt ashamed when he remembered what he had done to survive.

I find the same contradiction in Primo Levi's attitude toward his Auschwitz tattoo. "At a distance of forty years, my tattoo has become a part of my body," he wrote in *The Drowned and the Saved*. "I don't glory in it, nor am I ashamed of it, I do not display and do not hide it. I show it unwillingly to those who ask out of pure curiosity; readily, and with anger, to those who say they are incredulous." The victim remains a victim, Levi steadfastly maintained, not because he wanted to be identified as one but because he was driven to assert his innocence, the utter innocence of all who suffered and died in the death camps. More specifically he felt compelled to oppose the premise of the film *The Night Porter*, that camp inmates unconsciously collaborated with their oppressors, a suggestion in line with Bettelheim's claim that *shtetl* Jews had a hand in their own destruction. Such logic served to absolve the Germans of their responsibility for the Holocaust, Levi feared, and this he absolutely refused to support.

Levi counted himself among the survivors who needed to speak of their ordeal in order to live with their memories. "Often young people ask me why I don't have [my tattoo] erased, and this surprises me: why should I?" he demanded. "There are not many of us in the world to bear this witness." In his books as in the talks he gave in front of schoolchildren,

Levi adopted the calm, measured tone of the witness. Yet he assumed even this role with reluctance because he felt that it was not he but his dead companions who were the true witnesses of Auschwitz. Death purified them even as it deprived them of the ability to speak for themselves, which was not true for Levi and his fellow survivors. "Coming out of the darkness, one suffered because of the required consciousness of having been diminished," he confessed in the essay he titled "Shame." "Not by our will, cowardice, or fault, yet nevertheless we had lived for months and years at an animal level." Inside the camps, the capacity for human solidarity was extinguished. The survivor knows this, knows that he lived while others died, "died not despite their valor," in Levi's anguished words, "but because of it." In the end, nothing he wrote or said or did could erase the shame he felt for having survived Auschwitz. "I felt innocent, yes, but enrolled among the saved and therefore in permanent search of justification in my own eyes and those of others."[15]

I have arrived at the still point at the center of Primo Levi's story, but knowing why he hated himself is not enough to relieve me of the burden of his suicide. Levi wrote, as he freely admitted, to awaken the moral conscience of his readers. Coldly, and with a scientist's attention to detail, he laid bare the brutal logic that governed the camps: the useless violence that served to degrade the victim while making it possible for the murderer to do his job. Reading him, we cannot pretend not to know how human beings come to be deprived of their dignity, nor can we close our eyes to the useless violence in the world around us. But if there is any lesson to be drawn from Primo Levi's writing, it is this: to succumb to anger, even righteous anger, is to diminish ourselves as human beings.

How, then, do we define ourselves in relation to suffering and injustice? The tragic artists and intellectuals who have intrigued me over the years all endeavored to answer this question. I suspect their suicides were linked to their failure, ultimately, to resolve it. Samson, in the book of Judges, called on God to avenge him against his tormentors. We are told how he found the strength to pull the temple of the Philistines down upon himself, killing his enemies at the cost of his own life: "And Samson said, 'Let me die with the Philistines.'" Weil's martyrdom, Plath's self-pity, Arbus's relentless pursuit of ugliness—all derived from a similar, biblical urge. The same quest for absolutes, the longing for perfection that drove them to create, also contributed to their destruction.

With Bettelheim, the desire for retribution was foremost. Toward the end of *The Informed Heart*, his analysis of the psychological effects of the concentration camps, he poses the question of why more Jews did not fight back in the manner of Samson. "Why," he wonders, "did so few of the millions of prisoners die like men?" To answer this question he brings in a story first related by Eugen Kogon, a German political prisoner who documented some of the worst atrocities committed in the death camps. A Jewish woman, a former dancer, just instants away from being sent to the gas chamber, was commanded by an SS officer to dance naked in front of him. "She did, and as she danced, she approached him, seized his gun, and shot him. She too was immediately shot to death. But isn't it probable," Bettelheim asks, "that despite the grotesque setting in which she danced, dancing made her once again a person?"[16] Dignity, identity, and protest are all bound up in Bettelheim's account of the dancer's suicide. Coming where it does in his book, the story is more than an argument in favor of fighting back. An example of "supreme self-assertion," it serves to resolve the dilemma of the Holocaust as Bettelheim saw it, pointing the way out of the hopelessness that caused the millions to march to their deaths. The terrible beauty of the gesture lay in its inevitability. As an artistic statement—and we are clearly in the realm of performance—the dancer's death restores power to the brutalized victims of Nazi oppression. What better way to reclaim her freedom than to die on her own terms?

But we need to remind ourselves that this is not art. It is a real woman's death under unimaginably horrible circumstances. In Kogon's book the story of the dancer comes in the middle of a long paragraph of cruelties witnessed by a Czech member of the service squads, chilling evidence of the sadism of the Auschwitz guards. The event merits three sparse sentences; the dancer was shot unceremoniously and her fellow prisoners were herded into the showers. A previous chapter describes the collective suicides of Dutch Jews at Mauthausen, hundreds of men who threw themselves into the quarry where they were being worked to death. "When new batches of Jewish prisoners arrived, the SS had its fun by dubbing them 'parachute troops,' " Kogon reports.[17] There is nothing redemptive in these stories. For Bettelheim to derive hopeful lessons from a prisoner's suicide is the worst kind of fantasy—further evidence, it would appear, of his fairy-tale presumptions. But he is in esteemed company. "The woman is perfected," Plath wrote six days before committing suicide. "Her dead body wearing the smile of accomplishment." Such perfection exists only in poetry. The tragedy in some artists' suicides is that they tried to convince themselves otherwise.

I have come full circle. Améry's suicide—the event with which I began—seems like a bitter echo of the dancer's death, at least in its Bettelheim version. Both deaths represent a heroic reclaiming of dignity by the degraded victims of Nazi persecution, the Pyrrhic culmination of their struggle to re-create meaning, to re-create themselves, by leaving the world on their own terms. But the lesson to be drawn from either case is not a positive one. Dying on your own terms is still dying. Améry said that in Auschwitz all the poetry and philosophy he used to love became worthless. He regretted this deeply, the loss of his humanity. The loss, that is, of everything he valued: the consolations of beauty, empathy, rationality, and truth. In their place grew fear and resentment, monstrous feelings that could not be expunged except through an extreme act of violence, an act of retribution directed not simply against society, but also—inexorably—against himself. "Often I have asked myself whether one can live humanly in the tension between fear and anger," Améry wrote.[18] Haunting words, and dreadfully relevant to today's world.

# Notes

## CHAPTER 1. DEFIANT DEATH

1. Jean Améry, *On Suicide: A Discourse on Voluntary Death*, John Barlow, tr. (Bloomington, Ind., 1999), 78–79.

2. Jean Améry, "Resentments," in *At the Mind's Limits. Contemplations by a Survivor on Auschwitz and Its Realities*, Sidney Rosenfeld and Stella P. Rosenfeld, tr. (Bloomington, Ind., 1980), 80.

3. Améry, *On Suicide*, 152.

4. Améry, *On Suicide*, 27.

5. Jean Améry, "In the Waiting Room of Death: Reflections on the Warsaw Ghetto," in *Radical Humanism*, Sidney Rosenfeld and Stella P. Rosenfeld, tr. (Bloomington, Ind., 1984), 28.

6. Améry, *On Suicide*, 121.

7. Honoré de Balzac, *The Wild Ass's Skin*, H. J. Hunt, tr. (Harmondsworth, England, 1977), 29.

8. Plato, *Phaedo*, in *The Death of Socrates*, Hugh Tredennick, tr. (London, 1969), 181.

9. St. Augustine, *City of God* (Garden City, N.Y., 1958), I, 57–61.

10. Michael MacDonald and Terence R. Murphy, *Sleepless Souls: Suicide in Early Modern England* (New York, 1990).

11. John Donne, *Biathanatos*, Ernest W. Sullivan II, ed. (Newark, Del., 1984), 29. I have modernized the English of Donne's text.

12. John McManners, *Death and the Enlightenment: Changing Attitudes Toward Death Among Christians and Unbelievers in the Eighteenth Century* (New York, 1981).

13. On the classicism of the Enlightenment, see: Peter Gay, *The Enlightenment: An Interpretation*, Volume I: *The Rise of Modern Paganism* (New York, 1966), 59–126.

14. Montesquieu, *Persian Letters*, C. J. Betts, tr. (Harmondsworth, England, 1973), 281.

15. Dorinda Outram, *The Body in the French Revolution: Sex, Class and Political Culture* (New Haven, Conn., 1989), 90–105.

16. E. Caro, "Du Suicide dans ses rapports avec la civilization," in *Nouvelles études morales sur le temps présent* (Paris, 1869), 23.

17. M. Reydellet, *Du Suicide considéré dans ses rapports avec la morale publique et le progrès de la liberté dans les pays anciens et modernes mais surtout en France* (Paris, 1820), 79. Antoine Caillot, *Mémoires pour servir à l'histoire des moeurs et des usages des Français* (Paris, 1827), 355. Saint-Marc Girardin, "Du Suicide et de la haine de la vie," in *Cours de littérature dramatique ou de l'usage des passions dans la drame*, deuxième éd. (Paris, 1845), 76.

18. Ch. F. Sol, *Le Suicide considéré dans son principe et ses rapports avec l'état social* (Paris, 1842), 18.

19. J. Tissot, *De la Manie du suicide et de l'esprit de révolte, de leurs causes et de leurs remèdes* (Paris, 1840), v–vi, 8.

20. For a summary of this literature, see Jan Goldstein, *Console and Classify: The French Psychiatric Profession in the Nineteenth Century* (Cambridge, England, 1997), 1–7.

21. Louis Florentin Calmeil, *De la Folie considéré sous le point de vue pathologique, philosophique, historique et judiciare* (Paris, 1845), 13. G. F. Etoc-Demazy, "Sur la Folie dans la production du suicide," *Annales médico-psychologiques*, 1st ser., no. 7 (1846), 341.

22. "Sur le Suicide," in *Napoleon Wrote Fiction*, Christopher Frayling, tr. and ed. (New York, 1971), 77. General Count Montholon, *History of the Captivity of Napoleon at St. Helena* (Philadelphia, 1846), III, 66–68.

23. Montholon, *History*, III, 68.

24. C. E. Bourdin, "Le Suicide, est-il toujours le résultat ou, si l'on veut, le symptôme d'un trouble d'esprit? En d'autre termes, le suicide est-il toujours une maladie?" *Annales médico-psychologiques*, VIII (1846), 43.

25. J. E. D. Esquirol, "Suicide," *Grand dictionnaire des sciences médicales* (Paris, 1821), 282.

26. *La République*, 1 juillet 1848; *L'Union*, 12 novembre 1865; *La Petite république*, 1 and 6 janvier 1893. On the medicalization of social disorders, see Robert Nye, *Crime, Madness, and Politics in Modern France: The Medical Concept of National Decline* (Princeton, 1984).

27. Biaute, "Mélancholie suicide consécutive à l'onanisme," *Annales médico psychologiques*, VIII (1888), 34–39.

28. For a discussion of the personal and professional anxieties out of which the entire nineteenth-century crusade against masturbation derived, see Peter Gay, *The Bourgeois Experience: Victoria to Freud*, Volume I: *Education of the Senses* (New York, 1984), 294–318.

29. Quetelet, *Sur L'homme et le développement de ses facultés, ou essai de physique sociale* (Paris, 1835), 2 vols.

30. A. M. Guerry, *Essai sur la statistique morale de la France* (Paris, 1833) 11, 69. Ian Hacking, *The Taming of Chance* (Cambridge, England, 1990), 79.

31. M. Brouc, "Considérations sur les suicides de notre époque," *Annales d'hygiène publique et de médecine légale*, XVI (1836) 224. Egiste Lisle, *Du Suicide, statistique, médecine, histoire et legislation* (Paris, 1856), 293–294, 473. Dr. Vacher, "La mortalité a Paris en 1872," *Journal de la société de statistique de Paris* (1874), 103. Félix Voisin, "De L'identité de quelques-unes des causes du suicide, du crime et des maladies mentales," *Bulletin de l'académie de medicine*, I (1872), 413, 414.

32. Emile Durkheim, *Suicide: A Study in Sociology*, John A. Spaulding and George Simpson, tr. (New York, 1951), 212, 278–280, 332.

33. Durkheim, *Suicide*, 249, 250.

34. Durkheim, *Suicide*, 387.

35. *La Reforme industrielle,* 6 février 1833. *Le Populaire,* 5 juin 1842.

36. Durkheim, *Suicide,* 151.

37. Améry, "On the Necessity and Impossibility of Being a Jew," in *At the Mind's Limits,* 100.

38. Améry, *On Suicide,* 121.

CHAPTER 2. DEATH AND DEMOCRACY

1. *France-Soir,* 5 August 1982.

2. Claude Buillon and Yves Le Bonniec, *Suicide, mode d'emploi: Histoire, technique, actualité,* 4th ed. (Paris, 1987), 11.

3. Derek Humphry, *Final Exit: The Practicalities of Self-Deliverance and Assisted Suicide for the Dying* (Eugene, Ore., 1991).

4. Humphry, *Final Exit,* 105.

5. Buillon and Bonniec, *Suicide, mode d'emploi,* 44.

6. See Peter Filene's excellent study, *In the Arms of Others: A Cultural History of the Right-to-Die in America* (Chicago, 1998).

7. For a discussion of the popular reception of *The Nouvelle Héloïse,* see Robert Darnton, "Readers Respond to Rousseau," in *The Great Cat Massacre and Other Episodes in French Cultural History* (New York, 1984).

8. Jean-Jacques Rousseau, *La Nouvelle Héloïse,* in *Oeuvres complètes* (Paris, 1964) II, 37, 53, 147, 148.

9. *Julie,* 378, 383, 393.

10. *Julie,* 527.

11. Daniel Mornet, *La Nouvelle Héloïse de Jean-Jacques Rousseau* (Paris, 1967), 30.

12. *La Nouvelle Héloïse* appeared in 1761 to great acclaim. *Emile* and *The Social Contract* were published a year later, and both were immediately banned by the government of Geneva, forcing Rousseau into exile.

13. Jean-Jacques Rousseau, *Du Contrat social,* in *Oeuvres complètes* (Paris, 1964), III, 365.

14. Rousseau, *Du Contrat social,* 406.

15. Rousseau, *Emile,* in *Oeuvres complètes* (Paris, 1964), IV, 290, 468, 469.

16. Rousseau, *Emile,* 856, 857.

17. Alexis de Tocqueville, *Democracy in America*, Henry Reeve, tr. (New York, 1945) I, 6, 9, 7.

18. Tocqueville, *Democracy* I, 8; II, 106; I, 7.

19. Robert F. Berkhofer, Jr., *The White Man's Indian: Images of the American Indian from Columbus to the Present* (New York, 1978), and Henry Nash Smith, *Virgin Land: The American West as Symbol and Myth*, 2nd ed. (Boston, 1970).

20. Tocqueville, *Democracy*, I, 346–347, 24.

21. Ibid., I, 240, 369.

22. Ibid., II, 355, 358, 348.

23. Ibid., I, 15.

24. For a feminist perspective on *Atala*, see the essays by Naomi Schor, Margaret Waller, Marie-Claire Vallois, and Madelyn Gutwirth in Sara E. Melzer and Leslie W. Rabine, eds., *Rebel Daughters: Women and the French Revolution* (Oxford, 1992).

25. Chateaubriand, *Atala, René, Les Aventures du dernier abencérage* (Paris, 1962), 118.

26. Ibid., 82, 122–123.

27. Ibid., 123, 128.

28. Ibid., 162.

29. Ibid., 165–166.

30. Ibid., 165.

31. Text from the label beside the painting in an exhibition on the American Sublime at London's Tate Gallery, February 21–May 19, 2002.

32. Tocqueville, *Democracy*, I, 347–348.

33. Ibid., I, 347.

## CHAPTER 3. SEX AND SUICIDE

1. Edward Thompson, *Suttee* (London, 1928), 42.

2. John Stratton Hawley, ed., *Sati: The Blessing and the Curse. The Burning of Wives in India* (Oxford, 1994), "Introduction," 11–13. I have benefited from the articles in this collection in my discussion of *Sati*. Thompson, 78.

3. Allan Bloom, *The Closing of the American Mind: How Higher Education Has*

*Failed Democracy and Impoverished the Souls of Today's Students* (New York, 1987), 26.

4. Spivak's quip appeared in a now-famous article, "Can the Subaltern Speak?: Speculations on Widow-Sacrifice." First published in *Wedge* (Winter/Spring 1985), 120–130, and later included in an anthology edited by Cary Nelson and Lawrence Grossberg, *Marxism and the Interpretation of Culture* (Urbana, Ill., 1988), 271–313, it has recently been revised. See the debate over the 1987 *sati* committed by Roop Kanwar in Rajasthan in Hawley, *Sati*, 101–186.

5. Catherine Weinberger-Thomas found "an ocean of stories" of modern India in the British Parliamentary Papers on widow-burning in India, published in London between 1821 and 1830. See *Ashes of Immortality: Widow Burning in India*, Jeffrey Mehlman and David Gordon White, tr. (Chicago, 1999), 131.

6. Cited in Thompson, *Suttee*, 113.

7. Dorothy M. Figueira, "Die Flambierte Frau: Sati in European Culture," in Hawley, *Sati*, 57–63.

8. "The Trial of 'Madame Bovary': Speech for the Defense," and "Verdict," reprinted in Gustave Flaubert, *Madame Bovary*, Mildred Marmur, tr. (New York, 1964), 348, 351, 357, 402.

9. Flaubert, *Madame Bovary*, 51, 153.

10. Ibid., 262, 266.

11. Charles Baudelaire, "Madame Bovary," in *Oeuvres complètes* (Paris, 1976), II, 82, 83. In "The Uses of Male Hysteria: Medical and Literary Discourse in Nineteenth-Century France," *Representations* 34 (1991), 134–165, Jan Goldstein explores the implications of Madame Bovary's androgyny for Flaubert himself.

12. Jules Barbey D'Aurevilly, "M. Gustave Flaubert," in *Critical Essays on Gustave Flaubert*, Laurence M. Porter, ed. (Boston, 1986), 52, 53.

13. For much of the nineteenth century, girls' education emphasized these virtues. See Rebecca Rogers, "Boarding Schools, Women Teachers, and Domesticity: Reforming Girls' Secondary Education in the First Half of the Nineteenth Century," *French Historical Studies* 19 (Spring 1995), 152–181.

14. Barbey, "M. Gustave Flaubert," 55.

15. *Le Procès de Madame Lafarge* (Paris, 1840), 405. Quoted in Mary S. Hartman, *Victorian Murderesses: A True History of Thirteen Respectable French and English Women Accused of Unspeakable Crimes* (New York, 1976), 34, 14, 37.

16. Quoted by Michelle Perrot in her essay "The Family Triumphant," in *A History of Private Life*, Perrot, ed., 105.

17. Alexandre Dumas *fils*, *L'Homme-Femme. Réponse à M. Henri D'Ideville*, 7th ed. (Paris, 1872), 174, 54, 51.

18. Eugène Poitou, *Du Roman et du théâtre contemporains et de leur influence sur les moeurs*, 2nd ed. (Paris, 1858) 128, 200, 72.

19. Gustave Flaubert, *Flaubert in Egypt: A Sensibility on Tour*, Francis Steegmuller, ed. and tr. (New York, 1979), 110.

20. Charles Bourdin, *Du Suicide considéré comme maladie* (Batignolles, 1845), 54; Alexandre Brierre de Boismont, *Du Suicide et de la folie suicide considéré dans leur rapports avec la statistique, la médecine et la philosophie* (Paris, 1856), 118.

21. Brierre, *Du Suicide*, 23–27.

22. Alexandre Parent-Duchâtelet, *La Prostitution à Paris au XIXième siècle*, Alain Corbin, ed. (Paris, 1981).

23. Flaubert, *Madame Bovary*, 294, 307.

24. "The Trial of 'Madame Bovary': Speech for the Defense," 351, 357, 348.

25. Leo Tolstoy, *Anna Karenina* (Harmondsworth, England, 2001), 638.

26. Ibid., 751, 766, 767.

27. Ibid., 780, 781.

28. Montesquieu, *Persian Letters*, 281.

29. Germaine de Staël, *Corinne, or Italy*, Avriel H. Goldberger, tr. (New Brunswick, N.J., 1987), 357, 261.

30. Ibid., 124, 301, 330.

31. Ibid., 315.

32. Ibid., 272, 419.

33. George Sand, *Lélia* (Paris, 1960), 48.

34. Ibid., 48, 95, 172.

35. Ibid., 60, 216–217, 207.

36. Ibid., 96, 324.

37. Richard Wagner, "The Twilight of the Gods," in *The Ring of the Nibelung*, Stewart Robb, tr. (New York, 1960), 339.

38. Carl Dahlhaus, *Richard Wagner's Music Dramas*, Mary Whittall, tr. (Cambridge, England, 1979), 97.

### CHAPTER 4. LEAVING YOU

1. Balzac, *The Wild Ass's Skin*, 172–173.
2. Saint-Marc Girardin, "Du Suicide et de la haine de la vie," in *Cours de la littérature dramatique ou de l'usage des passions dans la drame*, 2nd ed. (Paris, 1845), 76.
3. [François Auguste René, Vicomte de] Chateaubriand, *Mémoires d'outre-tombe*, ed. nouvelle, Bibliothèque de la Pleiade, Maurice Levaillant, ed. (Paris, 1946), I, 100.
4. *René*, in *Oeuvres complètes de Chateaubriand* (Paris, 1861), III, 91; *Raphaël, Pages de la vingtième année*, in *Ouevres complètes de Lamartine* (Paris, 1863), XXXII, 194.
5. Victor Hugo, *Les Misérables*, Norman Denny, tr. (Harmondsworth, England, 1980), 409, 410, 402.
6. George Sand, *Lélia*, Maria Espinosa, tr. (Bloomington, Ind., 1978), 62, 226, 227.
7. Roland Barthes, *A Lover's Discourse*, Richard Howard, tr., reprinted in Susan Sontag, ed., *Barthes: Selected Writings* (New York, 1982), 450.
8. AN: F7 9726, Hautes Pyrenées, report dated 12 April 1826.
9. Georges Minois, *History of Suicide: Voluntary Death in Western Culture* (Baltimore, 1999), 268.
10. Johann Wolfgang von Goethe, *The Sorrows of Young Werther and Novella*, Elizabeth Mayer and Louise Bogan, tr. (New York, 1990), 165.
11. Henri Blanchard, *De la mort volontaire ou considérations politiques et législatives sur le suicide* (Paris, 1855), 45–46; Saint-Marc Girardin, "Des sentiments qui accompagnent l'idée du suicide dans le théâter moderne," in *Cours de littérature dramatique*, 79; Louis Maigron, *Le Romantisme et les moeurs, Essai d'étude historique et sociale d'après des documents inédits* (Paris, 1910), 2, 10, 35, 313.
12. Balzac, *The Wild Ass's Skin*, 29.
13. Richard Friedenthal, *Goethe: His Life and Times*, (London, 1965), 129, 131.

14. AN: F7 9810, Gironde, report dated 20 July 1816; AN: F7 9723, Ardennes, report dated 5 July 1825; AN: F7 9727, Meuse, report dated 5 January 1829; AN: F7 9810, Somme, report dated 25 July 1816.

15. AN: F7 9713, Jura, report dated 23 July 1817.

16. AN: F7 9719, Pas de Calais, report dated 9 October 1820.

17. AN: F7 9723, Drôme, report dated 12 August 1825; AN: F7 9714, Nord, report dated 10 December 1817; AN: F7 9719, Oise, report dated 14 February 1821.

18. AN: F7 9718, Puy de Dôme, report dated 20 May 1820; AN: F7 9718, Meuse, report dated 10 April 1823; AN: F7 9726, Rhône, report dated 15 July 1819.

19. André Imberdis, Le Dernier jour d'un suicidé (Paris, 1835), 15.

20. AN: F7 9722, Aube, report dated 16 February 1829; AN: F7 9722, Ardennes, report dated 14 May 1824; AN: F7 9718, Lyères, report dated 3 June 1816.

21. Cited in Albert Bayet, Le Suicide et la Morale (Paris, 1922), 769.

22. Cited in Louise J. Kaplan, The Family Romance of the Imposter-Poet Thomas Chatterton (Berkeley, Calif., 1987), 17–18.

23. Plato, Phaedrus, Walter Hamilton, tr. (Harmondsworth, England, 1973), 55–56.

24. Support for this interpretation may be found in Donald Smalley, ed., Browning's Essay on Chatterton (Cambridge, Mass., 1948). See especially the discussion of Browning's comparison of Chatterton with Shelley, 32–37.

25. Kaplan, Chatterton, 139, 186.

26. Cited in Bayet, Le Suicide, 749.

27. Philippe Auguste Villiers de l'Isle-Adam, Axël, June Guicharnaud, tr. (Englewood Cliffs, N.J., 1970), 183.

28. AN: F7 9728, Seine et Marne, report dated May/June 1827.

29. AN: F7 9728, Haute Vienne, report dated 18 September 1828; AN: F7 9716, Cher, report dated 5 March 1820; AN: F7 9721, Sarthe, report dated 25 June 1823.

30. Alexandre Brierre de Boismont, Du Suicide et de la folie suicide, 2nd ed. (Paris, 1865), x–xi, 165, 54, 74–93, 248, 267.

31. M. Reydellet, Du Suicide considéré dans ses rapports avec la morale publique

*et les progrès de la liberté dans les pays anciens et modernes mais surtout en France* (Paris, 1820), 6; Adelaide Celliez, *Les Anciens et les Français, ou veritables beautés de l'histoire de France et des Bourbons* (Paris, 1822), 15.

32. Durkheim, *Suicide*, 279–283.

33. Foreword to the Mayer and Bogan translation of *The Sorrows of Young Werther*, ix.

34. An excellent discussion of Durkheim's "Scientific Rationalism" may be found in Steven Lukes, *Emile Durkheim, His Life and Work: A Historical and Critical Study* (Stanford, Calif., 1985), 72–76.

35. Review of Alvarez, *The Savage God*, in *New York Times Book Review*, April 16, 1972.

36. William Styron, *Darkness Visible: A Memoir of Madness* (London, 1991), 81, 82, 79, 65, 35, 84.

37. Kay Redfield Jamison, *An Unquiet Mind: A Memoir of Mood and Madness* (London, 1997), 5, 92; Jamison, *Night Falls Fast: Understanding Suicide* (London, 2000), 180, 365–366, n. 181.

38. Alfred Alvarez, *The Savage God: A Study of Suicide* (London, 1971), 198, 32, 18.

## CHAPTER 5. TRAGIC ARTISTS

1. Patricia Bosworth, *Diane Arbus: A Biography* (London, 1985), 279, 131.

2. Susan Sontag, *On Photography* (New York, 1977), 37.

3. Bosworth, *Arbus*, 234.

4. Ibid., 318.

5. Simone Pétrement, *Simone Weil: A Life* (New York, 1976), 244, 314; Siân Miles, ed., *Simone Weil: An Anthology* (London, 1986), 29.

6. Miles, *Weil*, 41.

7. Bosworth, *Arbus*, 321.

8. Pétrement, *Weil*, 509.

9. Paula Bennett, *My Life a Loaded Gun: Female Creativity and Feminist Politics* (Boston, 1986).

10. The earliest version of this theory, to my knowledge, was Alfred Alvarez's in *The Savage God*, 31.

11. Richard Pollak, *The Creation of Dr. B: A Biography of Bruno Bettelheim* (New York, 1997).

12. Bruno Bettelheim, "Freedom from Ghetto Thinking," *Freud's Vienna and Other Essays* (New York, 1990), 269.

13. Bettelheim, "Children of the Holocaust" in *Freud's Vienna*, 218.

14. John Updike review of *The Uses of Enchantment*, *New Yorker*, December 13, 1976, 163.

15. Primo Levi, *The Drowned and the Saved*, Raymond Rosenthal, tr. (London, 1995), 95, 13, 56, 63, 101.

16. Bruno Bettelheim, *The Informed Heart: A Study of the Psychological Consequences of Living Under Extreme Fear and Terror* (London, 1986), 264, 265.

17. Eugen Kogon, *Der SS-Staat* (Stockholm, 1947), 180. I have relied on Heinz Norden's translation in the 1973 English edition of Kogon's book, *The Theory and Practice of Hell: The German Concentration Camps and the System Behind Them* (New York, 1973), 167, for the story of the Dutch Jews at Mauthausen.

18. Améry, "On the Necessity and Impossibility of Being a Jew," 100.

# Index

Abuse of euthanasia, 41
Accident vs. suicide, 12–13. *See also* Concealment of suicide by families.
Adkins, Janet, 41–42
Adultery, 70–89; as political protest, 75–79, 86; punishment by suicide in literature, 82–89
Affront, suicide as, 112. *See also* Rebellion, suicide as; Revenge; Selfishness, suicide as; Threat, suicide as.
Alvarez, Alfred, 128
Ambition as a cause of suicide, 122–124
Améry, Jean, 3–7, 9, 29–30, 36–37, 153
Anger, xi, 3–4, 137–142, 148–

150, 153. *See also* Rebellion, suicide as; Revenge.
*Anna Karenina* (Tolstoy), 83–84
Anti-psychiatry movement, 22–23
Anti-semitism, 137–138, 144–145, 149. *See also* Holocaust victims.
Antony, Mark, 9
Arbus, Diane, 133–134, 137, 138
Art: portraying Native Americans, 63; portraying suicides, 115
Artists. *See* Misunderstood genius; Tragic artists; Tragic figures.
*Atala* (Chateaubriand), 59–63
Auden, W. H., 124
Augustine (Saint), 10–11, 13
Avedon, Richard, 137
*Axël* (Villiers de l'Isle-Adam), 117–118

Balzac, Honoré de, 7, 95–96, 104

Barbey d'Aurevilly, Jules, 74–75, 76

Baudelaire, Charles, 73–74

Bennett, Paula, 139

Bettelheim, Bruno, 143–148, 151

*Biathanatos* (Donne), 14

Biaute, Dr., 28–29

Blanchard, Henri, 103

Bloom, Allan, 68–69

Bonald, Louis de, 76

Bourdin, Charles, 26–27, 79–80

Brierre de Boismont, Alexandre, 79–81, 85–86, 119–122

Brouc, Dr. M., 33

Brutus, 9

Buff, Charlotte, 105–106

Burial of suicides, 13–14

"Burning the Letter" (Plath), 139

Caillot, Antoine, 19

Calas, Jean, 16

Calmeil, Louis Florentin, 24–25

Cato, 9, 17–18, 43–44

Celliez, Adelaide, 122–123

Chateaubriand, François René, 59–63, 96–97, 124

Chatterton, Thomas, 114–117

*Chatterton* (Vigny), 114

"Children of the Holocaust" (Bettelheim), 146–147

Christianity: converts, 60–62, 135–137; and democracy, 58–59; medical views on suicide compared to, 24–25; passion compared to, 59–63, 92; rulings on suicide, 10–15, 61; sociological views on, 135

City life and suicide, 32–33

Civil liberty, 50–51. *See also* Democracy.

Class distinctions: artists' attempts to bridge, 133–138; and suicide, 118–122

Cleopatra, 9

Cole, Thomas, 63

Coleridge, Samuel Taylor, 114–115

Colonization: of India by Europeans, 67–70; of Native Americans by Europeans, 55–66

Comte, Auguste, 30

Comte, Josephine, 108, 109

Concealment of suicide by families, 16. *See also* Accident vs. suicide.

Cooper, James Fenimore, 63

*Corinne* (de Staël), 86–90

Cottle, Joseph, 117

*Creation of Dr. B, The* (Pollak), 144, 145

Creative self-expression, suicide as, 92, 94, 104, 114, 151, 153; literary allusions in actual suicides, 98, 100–114, 122–123. *See also* Free will; Rebellion, suicide as; Revenge; Self-determination and suicide.

Croft, Herbert, 115, 116

*Darkness Visible* (Styron), 125–127

Death as revenge, 89–90

*Death of Chatterton, The* (Wallis), 115

Defiance, suicide as, 3–37. *See also* Insanity; Political protest, suicide as.

Delamotte, Noel, 107
Democracy, 38–66; eighteenth-century ideals, 44–53; euthanasia and, 9, 38–42; isolation and, 54–55; nineteenth-century ideals, 53–66; religion and, 58–59; in the United States, 51, 53–66. *See also* French Revolution.
*Democracy in America* (Tocqueville), 53–66
Denmark, suicide rates, 19
"Der Gott un die Bjadere" (Goethe), 70
Desecration of suicides, 13–14
Diabolic possession, suicide as, 13–14
Disapproval of suicides, 111–112; class distinctions among, 118–122
Divine madness, 115–117, 125–129
Divine sanction of self-destruction, 10–11, 24. *See also* Martyrs.
Domestic violence and suicide, 79–82
Donne, John, 14
*Drowned and the Saved, The* (Levi), 149
*Du Suicide et de la folie suicide* (Brierre de Boismont), 119–122
Duchesne, Etienne, 111–112
Dumas, Alexandre *(fils)*, 77
Durkheim, Emil, 32, 34–35, 123–125

Eden, W. F., 70
"Edge" (Plath), 140

Eighteenth century: democratic ideals, 44–53; public debate on suicide, 15–18. *See also* French Revolution.
*Emile* (Rousseau), 51–53
England: public debate on suicide, 14; seventeenth century, 14
Esquirol, J. E. D., 27
*Essai sur la statistique morale de la France* (Guerry), 32–33
Etoc-Demazy, Gustave François, 25
Euphemisms, 40
Euthanasia, 9, 38–42. *See also* Terminal illness and suicide.

Families: concealment of suicide by, 16; effect of suicides on, x, xi, 12–13, 108, 112, 130–131
*Final Exit* (Humphry), 40
Flaubert, Gustave, 71–76, 79, 82–83
Foucault, Michel, 23
Fourier, Charles, 20, 31
France, 14–40; anti-psychiatry movement, 22–23; French Revolution and attitudes toward suicide, 15–19, 22–23, 53–54; legal aspects of suicide, 15–16, 17–18; medical views of suicide, 19, 33–34, 79–82, 119–122; political views of suicide, 18–23; prefects' reports of suicides, 108–110, 111–112, 118–121; psychiatric views of suicide, 21–30; public

debate on suicide, 18–21; sociological views of suicide, 30–36; statistics, development of, 30–36; suicide rates, 18–19, 21, 32–33

Free will, 28, 29–30, 32–33, 66; suspicion of, 42. *See also* Rebellion, suicide as; Revenge; Self-determination and suicide; Volition, removal from suicide.

Freedom, 4–5, 43–44; as a burden, 48–53; as a danger, 57; Rousseauian ideas, 44–53; suicide as, 39. *See also* Democracy; Free will; Imprisonment; Political views of suicide.

French Revolution, 15–19, 22–23, 53–54

Gaillard, Adila, 101–102

Genius, misunderstood, 113–118, 122–129

Genocide of Native Americans, 55–66

Gifford, Stanford Robinson, 63

Girardin, Saint-Marc, 19–20, 96, 103–104

Glorification: of ancient Rome in Revolutionary France, 16–18; of suicide, 97–104, 129

Goethe, Johann Wolfgang von, 70, 102–103, 105–106, 124

*Götterdämmerung* (Wagner), 92–94

Greece (ancient), suicide laws of, 8, 11; Romantic inspiration by, 115

Guerry, A. M., 31, 32–33

Hemlock Society, 39, 40–42

Henry, Patrick, 43

Heroic suicide, 7–11, 20, 25–27, 85, 95–129. *See also* Creative self-expression, suicide as; Honor and suicide.

History: of psychiatric views of suicide, 21–30; of sociology, 30–31; of statistics, 30–36

Holocaust victims, 3–7, 9, 143–153

Honor and suicide, 9–10, 16–18, 120–121. *See also* Heroic suicide; Misunderstood genius; Religious aspects of suicide.

Hotlines. *See* Suicide hotlines.

How-to manuals, 38–40; misuse of, 41

Hughes, Ted, 139

Hugo, Victor, 98–99

Humphry, Derek, 39, 40–41

"Iliad, The, or the Poem of Force" (Weil), 136

Illness: suicide as, 7, 23–30; terminal illness and suicide, 9, 38–42, 66. *See also* Medical views of suicide; Weakness, suicide as.

Imprisonment, 4–5

India: European colonization of, 67–70; *sati,* 67–70

Indians. *See* Native Americans.

Industrial development and suicide, 32–33

*Informed Heart, The* (Bettelheim), 151–152

Insanity: diabolic possession, 13–14; divine madness, 115–117,

Insanity *(cont.)*
125–129; suicide as, 23–30,
79–82. *See also* Psychiatric
views of suicide; Therapeutic
views of suicide; Weakness,
suicide as.
Intellectuals. *See* Creative self-
expression, suicide as;
Misunderstood genius; Tragic
artists; *individuals by name.*
Isolation: democracy and, 54–55;
suicide and, 4

Jamison, Kay Redfield, 127–128
Jerusalem, Karl Wilhelm, 106
Jesus, 10–11
Judas, 10–11

Keats, John, 114
Kestner, Johann Christian, 105–
106
Kevorkian, Jack, 41–42
Kipling, Rudyard, 67
Kogon, Eugen, 151–152

*La Peau de chagrin* (Balzac), 7, 95–
96, 104
"Lady Lazarus" (Plath), 141–142
LaFarge, Marie, 75–76
Laffourcade, Monsieur, 101–102
Lamartine, Alphonse de, 82, 97,
123–124
*Landscape with Tree Trunks* (Cole),
63
Laplace, Pierre-Simon, marquis
de, 30–31
*Last Day of a Suicide, The,* 112
*Last of the Mohicans* (Cooper), 63
"Last Suttee, The" (Kipling), 67

*Last Will and Testament*
(Chatterton), 116–117
*Le Suicide* (Durkheim), 123
Legal aspects of suicide:
eighteenth century, 15–16;
France, 15–16, 17–18; Greece
(ancient), 8, 11; Middle Ages,
11–13; religious rulings
compared to, 10–16; Rome
(ancient), 11–12
*Lélia* (Sand), 90–92, 99–100
*Les Misérables* (Hugo), 98–99
Levi, Primo, 149–151
Liberty: Rousseauian ideas, 44–
53. *See also* Free will;
Freedom; Self-determination
and suicide; Volition, removal
from suicide.
Lisle, Egiste, 33–34
Literature: effect on actual
suicides, 98, 100–114, 122–
123; European literature on
Native Americans, 53–66;
literary suicides, 45–53, 59–
63, 70–89, 91–92, 97–104,
111, 117–118, 123–124;
memoirs of depression, 127–
129; as revenge, 106;
theatrical suicides, 14, 92–94;
tragic figures, 85, 97–104,
113; by women about women,
86–92. *See also* Literature on
suicide; Misunderstood genius;
Tragic artists; *individual works
by name.*
Literature on suicide: defenses of
suicide, 14, 25–26, 114–117;
how-to manuals, 38–40, 43;
medical, 33–34; political, 38–

40, 43, 44–66; statistical, 32–34. *See also* Psychiatric views of suicide.

*Love and Madness* (Croft), 115, 116

Lucretia, 9

*Madame Bovary* (Flaubert), 71–76, 79, 82–83

Maigron, Louis, 104

Marriage. *See* Sex and suicide; Wives.

Martyrs, 24–25, 136–137. *See also* Divine sanction of self-destruction; Honor and suicide.

Materialism as a cause of suicide, 33–34

Mead, Margaret, 58

Medical views of suicide, 24–25, 26–27, 33–34; France, 19, 33–34, 79–82, 119–122. *See also* Illness; Psychiatric views of suicide; Therapeutic views of suicide.

Mental illness. *See* Illness; Insanity; Psychiatric views of suicide; Therapeutic views of suicide.

Michelet, Jules, 20

Middle Ages, church policy on suicide, 11–13

Misunderstood genius, 113–118, 122–129. *See also* Tragic artists.

Montaigne, Michel de, 16

Montesquieu, Charles Louis de Secondat, 17, 86

Montholon, Charles Tristan, 26

Moral statistics. *See* Statistics.

Mornet, Daniel, 49

*My Life a Loaded Gun* (Bennett), 139

Napoleon Bonaparte, 25–27, 102, 105

Native Americans: colonization by Europeans, 55–66; European art portraying, 63; European literature portraying, 53–66

*Night Falls Fast* (Jamison), 127–128

Nineteenth century: democratic ideals, 53–66; prefects' reports of suicides, 108–110, 111–112, 118–121; public debate on suicide, 18–21; studies on suicide, x, 30–36; suicide rates, 18–19; treatment of suicides, 28–30; women and suicide, 67–94. *See also* Romanticism and suicide.

Notes (suicide). *See* Suicide notes.

*Nouvelle Héloïse, The* (Rousseau), 45–50, 105

Oates, Joyce Carol, 125

Parent-Duchâtelet, Alexandre, 81–82

Passion: passionate men and suicide, 85; passionate women and suicide, 67–94; rationality compared to, 48–53, 64–65, 80–81, 83–84, 88; religion compared to, 59–63, 92; and repressed feelings, 87–88, 90–

Passion (*cont.*)
92, 146–148. *See also* Anger;
Romance and suicide;
Romanticism and suicide;
Tragic artists.
Pecqueur, Constantin, 20
Perfectionist ideals, 151–153
*Persian Letters* (Montesquieu), 17,
86
Philippou, Baron, 108–109
Philosophy on suicide, 19–20
Physician-assisted suicide, 41. *See
also* Terminal illness and
suicide.
Pinard, Ernest, 72
Plath, Sylvia, 128, 138–142, 152
Plato on Socrates, 7–9, 10, 115
Poitou, Eugène, 77–78
Police records of suicides, 100–
101. *See also* Prefects' reports
of suicides.
Political protest, suicide as, 4–9,
12–13, 16–22, 35–40, 43–44,
84, 151–153; adultery as, 75–
79, 86. *See also* Misunderstood
genius; Rebellion, suicide as;
Tragic artists.
Political views of suicide: anti-
psychiatry movement, 22–23;
conservative views, 18–24;
liberal views, 20, 22–23, 27,
35–36, 38–40, 43; literature,
38–40, 43, 44–66; psychiatry
influenced by, 21–24;
psychiatry's influence on, 27;
socialist views, 35–36. *See also*
Class distinctions; Democracy;
French Revolution.
Pollak, Richard, 145, 146, 147
Portia, 9

Poverty as a cause of suicide, 35–
36, 121
Prefects' reports of suicides, 108–
110, 111–112, 118–121. *See
also* Police records of suicides.
Prostitution, sociological views
of, 81–82
Psychiatric views of suicide: anti-
psychiatry movement, 22–23;
Christian views compared to,
24–25; history of, 21–30;
political agendas and, 21–24;
treatment of suicides, 28–30.
*See also* Medical views of
suicide; Therapeutic views of
suicide.
Public debate on suicide:
eighteenth century, 15–18;
England, 14; France, 15–21;
nineteenth century, 18–21;
seventeenth century, 14

Quetelet, Adolphe, 31–32

Rage. *See* Anger; Passion;
Rebellion, suicide as; Revenge.
Ragor, Augustine, 112–113
Raphaël (Lamartine), 97, 123–
124
Rational suicide, 40–41
Rationality: passion compared to,
48–53, 64–65, 80–81, 83–84,
88; of suicides, 4. *See also*
Heroic suicide; Political
protest, suicide as;
Romanticism and suicide;
Volition, removal from suicide.
Rebellion, suicide as, xi, 5, 11–
14, 111–113, 117–119. *See*

*also* Ambition as a cause of
suicide; Anger; Misunderstood
genius; Political protest,
suicide as; Selfishness, suicide
as; Threat, suicide as.
Reboul, Barthelemy, 110
Refinement and suicide, 117–122
Religious aspects of suicide:
Christian rulings, 10–15;
desecration of suicides, 13–14;
divine sanction of self-
destruction, 10–11, 24; legal
aspects compared to, 16; loss
of religion and suicide, 33–34;
saints and martyrs, 24–25,
136–137; sanctity of life, 41.
*See also* Christianity; Honor
and suicide.
*René* (Chateaubriand), 97, 124
Repressed feelings, 87–88, 90–
92, 146–148
Rescues from suicide, 3–4, 29.
*See also* Treatment of suicides.
Resistance in concentration
camps, 151–152
Resistance fighters (WWII), 5–6
Restraint of suicides, 28–29
Revenge, 5–6; death as, 89–90;
literature as, 106; suicide as, 5–
6, 84, 116–117, 122, 141. *See
also* Anger; Political protest,
suicide as; Rebellion, suicide
as; Selfishness, suicide as.
Reydellet, Pierre, 19
"Road to the Open, The"
(Améry), 4–5
Romance and suicide: in history,
108–112; in literature, 45–53,
59–63, 85, 91–92, 102–103,

117–118. *See also* Passion;
Romanticism and suicide; Sex
and suicide.
Romanticism and suicide, xii, 85,
95–129; actual suicides, 98,
100–114, 117–119; criticism
of, 119–129; glorification of
suicide, 97–104, 129; literary
suicides, 97–104, 111, 123–
124; memoirs of depression,
127–129; misunderstood
genius, 113–118, 122–129;
redemption by suicide, 92–94,
99–100; refinement and
suicide, 117–122; scripts for
suicide, 106–110; suicide
notes, 107–109, 110, 113,
116–117, 118, 120, 126;
weakness of suicides, 99. *See
also* Passion; Tragic artists.
Rome (ancient): as an analogy,
20, 34–35, 43–44, 135;
glorification of in
Revolutionary France, 16–18;
suicide laws, 11–12
Rousseau, Jean-Jacques, 43, 44–
53, 105

Saints, 24–25. *See also* Divine
sanction of self-destruction;
Honor and suicide; Martyrs.
Sand, George, 90–92, 99–100
*Sati,* 67–70, 92–94
Satires of suicide, 95–96
*Savage God, The* (Alvarez), 128
Saxony, suicide rates, 19
Scripts for suicide, 106–129
Self-determination and suicide, xi–
xii, 29–30, 151–153. *See also*

Self-determination . . . (cont.)
Creative self-expression,
suicide as; Free will; Political
protest, suicide as; Rebellion,
suicide as; Revenge; Volition,
removal from suicide.
Self-hatred, 134–138, 142–151
Selfishness, suicide as, 121–124.
See also Revenge; Social
responsibility and suicide.
Sellier, Felix, 101–102, 106–107
Seneca, 9
Seven Deadly Sins, The (Sue), 117
Sex and suicide: adultery and
suicide, 70–89; sati, 67–70.
See also Romance and suicide.
Shakespeare, William, 14
"Shame" (Levi), 150
Sin, suicide as, 12–13. See also
Religious aspects of suicide.
Social Contract, The (Rousseau),
50–51
Social disturbances as a cause of
suicide, 33–36
Social responsibility and suicide,
48–53, 103–104. See also
Selfishness, suicide as.
Socialist views on suicide, 35–36
Sociology: history of, 30–31;
literature, 44–66; travel and,
58; views of Christianity, 135;
views of prostitution, 81–82;
views of suicide, 30–36, 122–
125. See also Political views of
suicide.
Socrates, 7–9, 10, 115
Sontag, Susan, 133
Sorrows of Young Werther, The, 102–
103, 105–106, 124

Southey, Robert, 117
Staël, Germaine de, 86–90
Statistics: history of, 30–36;
literature on suicide, 32–34
Stoics, 9, 16–17, 19
Styron, William, 125–127
Sue, Eugène, 117
Suffering artist. See
Misunderstood genius; Tragic
artists; Tragic figures.
Suicide hotlines, 130–132
Suicide, mode d'emploi, 38–40, 43
Suicide notes, 107–109, 110,
113, 116–117, 118, 120, 126
Suicide rates: Denmark, 19;
France, 18–19, 21, 32–33;
Saxony, 19; sociological
studies, 32–33
Suttee. See Sati.
Sympathy for suicides, 108–110

Terminal illness and suicide, 9,
38–42, 66
Theatrical portrayals of suicide,
14, 92–94
Therapeutic views of suicide, 7.
See also Medical views of
suicide; Psychiatric views of
suicide.
Thomas Aquinas (Saint), 12
Thompson, Edward, 68
Threat, suicide as, xi, xii, 42–
44. See also Affront, suicide as;
Rebellion, suicide as; Revenge.
Tissot, Joseph, 21
Tocqueville, Alexis de, 43, 53–
66
Tolstoy, Leo, 83–84
Tragic artists, xii, 130–153;
anger, xi, 3–4, 137–142, 148–

150, 153; class distinctions and, 133–138; perfectionist ideals, 151–153; self-hatred, 134–138, 142–151; truth-seeking, 135–136. *See also* Creative self-expression, suicide as; Misunderstood genius; *individual artists by name.*

Tragic figures: Romantic literature, 85, 97–104; suicides' visions of themselves as, 113

Travel as an opportunity for social critique, 58

Treatment of suicides, 28–30. *See also* Rescues from suicide.

Truth, search for, 135–136

United States: democracy in, 51, 53–66; Native Americans, 55–66

*Unquiet Mind, An* (Jamison), 127–128

Updike, John, 147

Victims: suicides as, 140–141. *See also* Holocaust victims; Self-determination and suicide; Volition, removal from suicide; Weakness, suicide as.

Vigny, Alfred de, 113–114

Villiers de l'Isle-Adam, Philippe August, 117–118

Voisin, Félix, 34

Volition, removal from suicide, x–xi, xii, 28, 36, 42–43, 81. *See also* Free will; Self-determination and suicide.

Voltaire, 16, 17

Wagner, Richard, 92–94

Wallis, Henry, 115

Warsaw ghetto fighters, 5–6

Weakness, suicide as, 21, 99, 119–122

Weil, Simone, 134–138

Widows, *sati*, 68–70

*Wilderness, The* (Gifford), 63

Wives: adultery, 70–89; domestic violence and suicide, 79–82; men's literature on, 71–86; murder by, 75–76; punishment of immorality by suicide in literature, 82–89; rights of, 76–79, 87. *See also* Romance and suicide.

Women, 67–94; androgyny, 73–75; insanity, 79–82; prostitution, 81–82; self-repression, 87–88; tormented women, 85–86; unattainable women, 85, 90–92; women's literature on, 86–90. *See also* Wives.

Wordsworth, William, 114

Working class suicides, 118–122

Writers. *See* Creative self-expression, suicide as; Misunderstood genius; Tragic artists; *individuals by name.*

# A NOTE ON THE AUTHOR

Lisa Lieberman was born in Philadelphia and studied at the University of Pennsylvania and Yale University, where she received a Ph.D. in history. Her work, both fiction and nonfiction, has appeared in various journals, and she wrote the "Suicide" entry in the *Oxford Companion to the Body*. At present a Visiting Fellow at the University of East Anglia in England, Ms. Lieberman teaches modern European cultural and intellectual history at Dickinson College. She is married with three children.